THE CAT[illegible]E

J.D. Salinger

AUTHORED by J.J. Ross
UPDATED AND REVISED by Soman Chainani and Adam Kissel, October 10, 2008 and

COVER DESIGN by Table XI Partners LLC
COVER PHOTO by Olivia Verma and © 2005 GradeSaver, LLC

BOOK DESIGN by Table XI Partners LLC

Published by GradeSaver LLC, www.gradesaver.com

First published in the United States of America by GradeSaver LLC. 2009

ISBN 978-1-60259-199-8

Printed in the United States of America

For other products and additional information please visit

Table of Contents

Table of Contents

Biography of Salinger, J.D. (1919-)

Born in New York City on the first day of 1919, J.D. Salinger is the son of a Jewish father and a Christian mother. After brief periods of enrollment at both NYU and Columbia University, Salinger devoted himself entirely to writing, and by 1940 he had published several short stories in periodicals. Although his career as a writer was interrupted by World War II, Salinger returned from service in 1946 and resumed his career, writing primarily for *The New Yorker*. Some of his most notable stories include his first story for *The New Yorker*, "A Perfect Day for Bananafish" (1948), which tells of the suicide of a despairing war veteran, and "For Esmé--With Love and Squalor" (1950), which describes a U.S. soldier's encounter with two British children. Salinger has published a total of thirty-five short stories in various publications, including many in *The Saturday Evening Post*, *Story*, and *Colliers* between 1940 and 1948, and in *The New Yorker* from 1948 to 1965.

Salinger has continually enjoyed major critical and popular acclaim with *The Catcher in the Rye* (1951), the story of Holden Caulfield, a rebellious boarding-school student who attempts to run away from the adult world that he finds "phony." In many ways reminiscent of Mark Twain's *Adventures of Huckleberry Finn*, Salinger's only novel finds great sympathy for its wayward child protagonist. It drew from characters he had created in two short stories published in 1945 and 1946, "This Sandwich Has No Mayonnaise" and "I'm Crazy." The latter story is an alternate take on several of the chapters in *The Catcher in the Rye*.

Salinger was also very interested in Zen Buddhism, Hindu-Buddhism, and other Eastern beliefs. He drew increasingly from these traditions for his own work. Traces of Buddhism can be found throughout *Nine Stories*, for example, particularly in the book's closing story, "Teddy." Salinger also was a devoted student of *The Gospel of Sri Ramakrishna*, an important work of Hindu mysticism, translated by Joseph Campbell and Swami Nikhilananda.

Salinger followed *The Catcher in the Rye* with *Nine Stories* (1953), a selection of his best short stories, and *Franny and Zooey* (1961), which draws from two earlier stories in *The New Yorker*. In 1963 he published several of his short stories as a novel, *Raise High the Roof Beam, Carpenters*. He also published *Seymour: An Introduction*. His relatively small literary output and reclusive habits since that time have made Salinger the subject of great notoriety.

Since 1953, Salinger has resided in Cornish, New Hampshire, and claims that he continues to write. Although details about Salinger are notoriously vague because of his reclusiveness, he has become the subject of much speculation. He refuses to give interviews or to deal with the press. Personal information about Salinger is therefore limited but in great demand. Letters written by Salinger to a young woman with whom he had had an affair gained a $156,000 auction price at Sotheby's. In these letters, written in 1972, Salinger writes to Joyce Maynard, then an eighteen-year-old student at Yale, who later left college to live with Salinger for nine months. These letters trace his growing attachment to Maynard and deal with the necessity of guarding and protecting the writer's source of creativity from the glare of the outside world. Maynard later became a published writer herself, publishing the comic novel *To Die For* and, in a controversial move, publishing a memoir concerning her relationship with Salinger. In her memoir, Maynard implied that Salinger's demand for privacy stemmed from his awareness that his private activities, including several relationships with young women like Maynard, would ultimately mar his reputation.

About The Catcher in the Rye

Although J.D. Salinger has written many short stories, *The Catcher in the Rye* is Salinger's only novel and his most notable work, earning him great fame and admiration as a writer and sparking many high school students' interest in great literature. The protagonist's adventures and concerns about "phony" people engage readers young and old.

The novel draws on characters and themes that appeared in a number of Salinger's earlier short stories, some of which form the basis for individual chapters in *The Catcher in the Rye*. Indeed, the Caulfield family is the subject of two of Salinger's major stories, "This Sandwich Has No Mayonnaise" and "I'm Crazy," as well as a number of unpublished works.

The first of these stories, "This Sandwich Has No Mayonnaise," is narrated by Vincent Caulfield, who learns that his brother is missing from Pentey Preparatory School (changed to Pencey in the novel). Vincent serves as the basis for D.B. Caulfield, Holden's older brother in the novel, and is the protagonist in a number of stories by Salinger. In "An Ocean Full of Bowling Balls," Vincent recalls his relationship with Kenneth, his deceased younger brother (the obvious basis for Allie). This unpublished story also details how Kenneth becomes angry when an adult calls Holden crazy and how Holden complains about hypocritical adults at his summer camp.

Other Salinger stories can be read as filling in details left out of *The Catcher in the Rye*. "The Last and Best of the Peter Pans," narrated by Vincent Caulfield, focuses on a conversation between Vincent and his actress mother, Mary Moriarty, concerning a questionnaire from the draft board that she had hidden from Vincent. This conversation ends with a reference to her wanting to keep a child from going over a cliff, a notion that Holden references in *The Catcher in the Rye* when he discusses his ideal situation with Phoebe. In another story, "Last Day of the Last Furlough," Vincent and "Babe" Gladwaller prepare to go off to World War II. Salinger has Vincent Caulfield die during the war, and "The Stranger" concerns "Babe" Gladwaller's attempt to tell Vincent's girlfriend how he died.

The other major short story concerning the Caulfield family is "I'm Crazy," the story which forms the basis for the first two chapters of *The Catcher in the Rye* as well as the chapter in which Holden goes home to see Phoebe. In this story, however, Holden expresses greater regret for his expulsion from Pentey, even lamenting that he will never again play games of football on Saturday evenings with his friends from school. The chapter in which Holden tries to convince Sally to run away with him to New England finds its source in yet another short story, "Slight Rebellion Off Madison."

The derivation of *The Catcher in the Rye* from a series of unrelated short stories--as well as Salinger's affection for the form of the short story--helps explain the pacing and relative lack of narrative continuity in the novel. No setting or character other than Holden continues in the novel for more than two consecutive chapters (which also may be a characteristic feature of Holden's specific story). Holden, as narrator, is the only continuous character in the entire story. Characters such as Sally Hayes and Mr. Antolini appear only in one chapter and then mostly disappear. The first chapters of the novel, which are all set at Pencey, are the only ones that sustain the same characters and setting for an extended period. Furthermore, since Salinger reiterates thematic elements throughout the novel (in practically every chapter Holden complains about phonies), many of the chapters essentially could be short stories in themselves.

Character List

Holden Caulfield

The narrator and protagonist of *The Catcher in the Rye*, Holden is the son of a wealthy New York family who moves from boarding school to boarding school after being repeatedly expelled. Although he displays a number of typical teenage characteristics, his adolescent foibles become increasingly disturbing throughout the novel, revealing a self-destructive side. Holden, it seems, has been particularly devastated by the death of his brother Allie, who he considered the perfect child. This has thrown him into an existential crisis of sorts; he is unable to find joy in life or to cope with his loss. Ultimately on the brink, he capitulates to convention and comes back home, though there is little sense that he has found even the basic ingredients for happiness.

Phoebe Caulfield

Phoebe, Holden's nine-year-old younger sister, is more mature and intelligent than her age implies. She realizes the extent of her brother's misanthropy and unhappiness. Holden appreciates every minute detail of Phoebe's existence, it appears, including her stories about "Hazle Weatherfield, Girl Detective." Holden treats Phoebe with more respect and kindness than he treats any other character in the story. Phoebe, for her part, recognizes how tenuous Holden's grasp on reality is. Unlike her parents, she knows he is struggling, and she simply wants to be there for him. In the end, it is her willingness to go to the ends of the earth with him that wakes Holden up to the impossibility of his self-destructive impulses. He succumbs to this reality because he cannot bear to see Phoebe suffer.

Allie Caulfield

Holden's younger brother, Allie died from leukemia. Holden often reminisces about Allie, particularly about his baseball mitt, which Holden uses as the subject for Stradlater's essay. Holden adored Allie, but when Allie died, Holden lost his capacity to truly love without fear. The idea of putting his heart on the line for someone who might disappear has become Holden's crucible--and the consequences of shutting down have left him numb.

Mr. Antolini

Holden's former English teacher at Elkton Hills, Mr. Antolini now teaches at NYU. He allows Holden to stay with him and his wife after Holden leaves his home. He tells Holden that Holden is headed for a fall and that he envisions Holden dying nobly for an unworthy cause. When Holden awakens to find Mr. Antolini touching his head, he interprets it as a homosexual advance and quickly leaves the house. Holden says afterward that this type of perverse advance seems a regularity in his life.

Ward Stradlater

Vain, self-centered, and arrogant--nevertheless a "secret slob"--Stradlater is Holden's roommate at Pencey Prep. He asks Holden to write an English essay for him, but he gets angry after finding the essay too off-topic. Holden gets into a fight with Stradlater after he suspects that Stradlater seduced Jane Gallagher, with whom Holden is in love. At his core, Holden seems to want to be Stradlater and thus to command power over men and women alike.

Carl Luce

One of the most intelligent people Holden knows, Carl was a student at Whooton when Holden attended. Carl then went to Columbia. He meets Holden at the Wicker Bar, where he chastises Holden for his immature behavior and recommends that he get psychiatric help.

Robert Ackley

A boorish, obnoxious student at Pencey, Ackley lives in a dorm room connected to the one where Holden lives. He is socially inept and physically disgusting; his complexion is poor and Holden suspects that he never brushes his teeth.

Sally Hayes

Holden goes out on a date with Sally, whose pretentious mannerisms ultimately drive Holden to insult her. Despite his contempt for her, Holden asks her to run away with him to New England, where they would live in a cabin in the wilderness together. After he insults Sally, however, she breaks ties with him, and Holden oddly feels relieved about that.

Mr. Spencer

Holden's history teacher at Pencey, Mr. Spencer discusses Holden's expulsion with him before he leaves the school He advises Holden to find direction in his life.

Maurice

The elevator man at the Edmond Hotel who is also a pimp, Maurice assaults Holden after he refuses to pay a ten-dollar fee to the prostitute he has arranged for Holden. Maurice told Holden the charge would only be five dollars, but he later cheats him on the price--pummeling Holden after the boy argues for the original price.

Sunny

A prostitute whom Holden hires for the evening but then rejects. Sunny demands a ten-dollar payment, but Holden had been led to believe that the charge would only be five.

Bernice Krebs

Bernice is a blonde woman from Seattle whom Holden meets at the Lavender Room. Holden dances with Bernice but grows to dislike her because she displays too much enjoyment for being a tourist in New York City.

Faith Cavendish

Faith is a former burlesque stripper and supposed prostitute. Holden calls Faith late at night to set up a date, but she refuses to go.

Lillian Simmons

Lillian is one of D.B.'s old girlfriends. Holden meets her at Ernie's and promptly leaves to avoid her and her new boyfriend.

Lillian Antolini

The wife of Mr. Antolini, Lillian is an older woman who married Mr. Antolini because they shared similar intellectual interests.

Horwitz

Holden argues with Horwitz, a cab driver, on his way to Ernie's.

Jane Gallagher

Stradlater's date for the evening, Jane was a close friend of Holden several summers before. Holden frequently reminisces about spending time with her. Jane is one of the few people whom Holden speaks about in entirely positive terms; he is in love with her.

D.B. Caulfield

Holden's older brother, D.B. is a war veteran who is currently a screenwriter in Hollywood.

Selma Thurmer

The daughter of the Pencey headmaster, Selma is a nice girl, but Holden considers her unattractive because she does not treat her father with enough respect.

Dr. Thurmer

The headmaster of Pencey, Dr. Thurmer gives Holden advice that "life is a game" when he expels Holden from the school.

Mr. Haas

Mr. Haas is the Headmaster of Elkton Hills who, according to Holden, ignores "funny-looking" parents of Elkton students in favor of more elite parents.

Ossenburger

Ossenburger is a wealthy undertaker and Pencey graduate who gives a speech to the Pencey student body in which he exalts his relationship with Jesus.

Edgar Marsalla

Holden recounts that Edgar, a Pencey student, farted during the speech by Ossenburger.

Mr. Hartzell

An English teacher at Pencey, Mr. Hartzell is the only teacher who did not fail Holden during the previous semester.

Mal Brossard

Mal Brossard accompanies Holden and Ackley into the city to see a movie the night before Holden leaves Pencey.

Ernest Morrow

According to Holden, Ernest is "the biggest bastard that ever went to Pencey." Holden meets his mother on the train to New York and lies about how popular and respected Ernest is at school.

Rudolf Schmidt

Rudolf is the janitor at Pencey. Holden uses his name as a pseudonym when he talks to Mrs. Morrow on the train to New York.

Raymond Goldfarb

Holden remembers how he and this student at Elkton Hills got drunk together.

Dick Slagle

Dick is one of Holden's former roommates at Elkton Hills. Holden remembers him primarily because he had delapidated suitcases.

Al Pike

Al Pike is a former boyfriend of Jane Gallagher. Holden decries him as an arrogant student at Choate who presumably suffers from an "inferiority complex."

James Castle

Holden tells a story about how James Castle, a student at Elkton Hills, committed suicide by jumping out of his window after an argument.

Phil Stabile

According to Holden, James Castle committed suicide after an argument with Phil.

Major Themes

Painful Experience vs. Numbness

Perhaps the greatest theme of the novel involves the relationship between the pain of actual experience and feeling one's feelings, on the one hand, and on the other hand the equally devastating numbness that comes with shutting down one's emotions in order to avoid suffering. After the death of Allie, Holden essentially shuts down, forcing himself to lose all attachments to people so as never to be hurt again. He repeatedly mentions how important it is not to get attached to anyone, since this will lead to missing them once they are gone. By the end of the novel, he has spiraled so far down with this theory that he has become afraid to even speak to anyone. Phoebe is perhaps the only reminder that Holden still has the capacity to love. When he looks at her, he cannot help but feel the same tortured love that he felt for Allie. Nevertheless, the surges of these feelings leave him even more bereft. He knows he must leave Phoebe to protect himself, but when she shows up to accompany him on his journey, ultimately he puts his love for her first and sacrifices his own instinct to flee in order to return home.

Holden, it seems, is in the throes of an existential crisis. To a great degree he is numb to the pains and joys of life. Unable to come to terms with his brother's death, he has no one to show him the kind of parental or brotherly love that he himself gave Allie. Whenever someone does end up showing him even a hint of such love (such as Mr. Antolini), Holden ends up being disappointed.

Love and Sex

At his core, Holden is a deep, sensitive soul, at bottom unable to sublimate his feelings into numbness. He envies someone like Stradlater, who can simply pick up girls whenever he likes, and who treats sex as a casual pleasure. To Holden, however, sex is deeply discomforting. He cannot have it with girls he likes, and he cannot manage to numb himself enough to treat girls casually. Numbing himself to love, it seems, is Holden's greatest challenge. He feels too deeply about the world, about people, to truly shut down. When he finally does fall in love with Jane Gallagher, he soon discovers that Stradlater has a date with her, which confirms his suspicion that everything he loves eventually deteriorates. He leaves Pencey with some hope of inventing a new identity, but he cannot break out of his being. Even in the presence of a prostitute, he cannot think of having sex, only of having a conversation in the hope of feeling some glimmer of human affection with her. All Holden wants to do is talk, but he cannot find someone who will listen.

Loss of Innocence

Holden must face that fork in the road of adolescence when one realizes that maturity entails a loss of innocence—that greater knowledge of oneself and others and the circumstances all comes with a price. In Holden's case, he cannot bear to accept the death of Allie, the death of pure innocence that had no good reason to suffer or die. In Holden's eyes, Allie is truth, while everyone else is "phony." Innocence goes with idealism and a certain inability or unwillingness to bear and accept the harsher reality. Holden cannot bear to hold onto his innocence because innocence brings its own harms; people continue to disappoint him. Thus the cost of maturity is much less; innocence has been quite painful, too. Innocence has been problematic: the prostitute demands more money for nothing, the man who takes him in seems like a pedophile, and the cab drivers berate him as stupid when he asks simple questions about the birds in the park. While Allie's memory can help him preserve his innocence, this is not enough, for he cannot find real love in the outside world.

Besides, losing Allie has brought tremendous pain. Holden also has the common adolescent experience of perceiving that time in school learning mundane lessons feels petty when his entire soul is in flux as it comes to grips with reality. When the entire world around him appears phony, where can he go to grasp hold of some reality, some stable truth? Without an explanation why Allie was taken from him, there appears no reason behind the world's events, and in this respect Holden's maturity involves a deep loss of innocence such that he perceives that the reality of the world is its very irrationality.

Phoniness vs. Authenticity

Holden labels almost everyone a "phony," excepting Phoebe, Allie, and himself. In Holden's eyes, a "phony" is someone who embraces the world's mundane demands and tries to make something out of nothing—that is, just about everyone who studies in school or who puts on airs in order to do a job or achieve a goal. The fact that no one is acknowledging how trivial and fleeting life is, compared with the grand things we tell one another about reality—how difficult it is to truly love and share oneself with people knowing that all, like Allie, will eventually die—causes him to burn with frustration, even rage. Holden understands on some level one of the most profound truths of mortal life: the superficial matters little because it will not last, yet it is made to seem so much more important. Meanwhile, all around him, he must watch superficial people win honors through their artifice. He thus holds his deepest contempt for those who succeed as phonies: Stradlater, the Headmaster, and all the boys who treat school as if it is a club to be ruled by Social Darwinism. All Holden wants is some authentic living, to hold on to someone like Phoebe or Allie who knows nothing of the world's superficiality and therefore is not tainted by it, but he is afraid to make it too real out of the justified fear of one day losing them forever.

Life and Death

A key part of Holden's emotional life involves his reaction to Allie's death. People live for a while, but all too soon we all die. Allie did not choose it, but Holden thinks about James Castle, a skinny boy who jumped out the window at school and fell to his death. Holden himself entertains thoughts of a similar suicide. The decision to numb himself to his feelings about life is a decision to shut himself down emotionally so much that he is no longer truly living. It is a decision, however, that remains fundamentally impossible for Holden. When he thinks about James Castle, he cannot bear to imagine James just laying there amidst the stone and blood, with no one picking him up.

Holden might see some romance in suicide and some comfort in the idea that it ends internal pain, but death does seem worse, the ultimate loneliness. He seen the effects of death on the living as well. He thus cannot do to Phoebe what Allie has done to them already.

He plods on, only sure that he must gradually wean himself away from Phoebe so that she gets used to losing him forever--and so that he gets used to being away from her. Though Holden needs closeness and love in order to renew his life, he keeps driving himself further away from it in order to avoid the inevitable loss. The more he wants to experience life, the more antisocial he becomes and the more he imagines death. This paradox is part of Holden's life: there is pain in shutting down one's feelings, and there is pain in the risk of opening oneself up again. He impossibly tries to avoid pains that are inevitable for human mortals while they live.

Lack of Authority Figures

Holden is profoundly alone. His parents are absent except for insisting that he progress along a conventional path and stay in school as long as he can before he is kicked out or tires of each institution. His parents do not let him regroup but send him off to the next school. At Pencey, Holden finds no adult to trust with his feelings; most people everywhere are phony. Some adults even seem so selfish that they are willing to abuse children. Overall, Holden views adults with intense disappointment, even cynicism. How is it that the older they get, the farther from authenticity they get? Meanwhile, the gradual deterioration of the body disgusts him. Upon visiting an old professor, much of his thoughts are dedicated to the awfulness of the old man's body. There is no allure in growing older.

Authority does not seem related to wisdom, either. Adults tell Holden to find direction and thus stability, but he views such advice as both suspicious and naïve; playing such a game is inauthentic. Going his own way autonomously, as a law unto himself, does not work out so well either, so it is unclear where Holden might find legitimate authority.

Loneliness

Holden is very lonely, and his adolescent loneliness seems to run much deeper than the feelings so commonly felt at that age. He admits to his loneliness openly, and it gives him evidence that perhaps he might still have some emotions left. At the same time, Holden takes few steps to mitigate his loneliness. Whenever he feels the urge to meet someone, to call up a girl, to have a social experience, he ends up sabotaging it before he can get hurt. He thus protects himself so fully that he effectively shuts off any possibilities of alleviating his own loneliness. He might want to call Jane, for example, but he hangs up before she gets on the phone. He might want to sleep with a prostitute to feel human comfort, but this will not do. He might want to interact with friends at a bar, but he ends up saying something hurtful so that they abandon him. Pushing them away provides a deeper and deeper loneliness, but at these moments of choice he is willing to endure it rather than eventually face the ultimate, devastating loneliness of losing another person like Allie.

Glossary of Terms

"kills me"

Holden uses this term whenever something makes him feel pangs of love or similar emotion. For example, the notebooks of young kids "kill" him in that they push him to open up his hardened heart.

ace

top-quality, of the highest order

backasswards

completely wrong, misdirected, or out of order, so backwards that the rear or "ass" is at the fore

Benedict Arnold

perhaps the most famous traitor in American history, a man who fled from the American side during the Revolutionary War in order to give information to the British

bourgeois

pertaining to the phony, middle-class or better lifestyle

Brown Betty

an American dessert of baked pudding that dates back to colonial times

caddy

person who accompanies a golfer on the course and carries his bag of clubs, sometimes giving advice about a shot

Canasta

a card game similar to Rummy in which the object is to score the most points by creating melds of cards of the same rank, playing cards out of one's hand onto the table, eventually playing out all of one's cards

chiffonier

similar to a sideboard, a type of furniture with drawers that serves as a receptacle for odds and ends

cockneyed

shifted to one side

dough

money (slang)

earlap
the flap on a hunter's hat that covers one's ear to protect it from the weather

falsies
artificial breast enhancers worn inside one's dress

flitty
appearing homosexual

Flys Up
a playground variation of baseball where whoever catches a fly ball gets the next turn at bat

furlough
a break in action or temporary leave of absence, usually in the military

get wise with
to make sexual advances

give her the time
to have intercourse with a female

Gladstone
type of luggage

grippe
influenza; the flu

halitosis
a condition of having bad-smelling breath

highball
an alcoholic drink usually involving whisky in a tall glass

louse
a contemptible person

neck
to kiss or make out

pacifist

a person who is against war and believes in peace as a matter of principle (Holden calls himself one)

Peter Lorre

a famous character actor

phony

anyone who is inauthentic; one who lives on the surface or subscribes to artifice (Holden believes that most adults are phonies)

prince

a "good guy"; someone who is valorous and noble

ratty

tattered, dilapidated

rubbernecks

people who turn their heads to watch something out of curiosity, especially when it is none of their business

rye

grass grown as a food crop, closely related to wheat and barley

shadow punching

boxing against an imaginary opponent

snowing

fooling; pulling the wool over someone's eyes

strong box

a safe for storing valuables

Tattersall

a cloth pattern

the Lunts

famous stage actors who drew large crowds

West Point

famous military academy in the United States

wooden press

a kind of case for a wooden tennis racket, which kept it from warping (prior to modern tennis rackets made of other materials)

Short Summary

Holden Caulfield, the narrator of *The Catcher in the Rye*, begins with an authoritative statement that he does not intend the novel to serve as his life story. Currently in psychiatric care, this teenager recalls what happened to him last Christmas. This story forms the basis for his narrative. At the beginning of his story, Holden is a student at Pencey Prep School, irresponsible and immature. Having been expelled for failing four out of his five classes, Holden goes to see Mr. Spencer, his history teacher, before he leaves Pencey. Mr. Spencer advises him that he must realize that "life is a game" and one should "play it according to the rules," but the sixteen-year-old, who has already left four private schools, dismisses much of what Spencer says.

Holden returns to his dormitory, where he finds Robert Ackley, an obnoxious student with a terrible complexion who will not leave Holden alone, and Ward Stradlater, Holden's roommate. Stradlater is conceited and arrogant, a "secret slob" who asks Holden to write an English composition for him. Stradlater prepares for a date with Jane Gallagher, a friend of Holden from several summers before, while Holden goes with Ackley and Mal Brossard into New York City to see a movie. When he returns, Holden writes the composition for Stradlater. It is about his brother's baseball mitt. Holden relates that his brother Allie died of leukemia several years ago and states that he broke all of the windows in his garage out of anger on the night that Allie died.

When Stradlater returns, he becomes upset at Holden for writing what he thinks is a poor essay, so Holden responds by tearing up the composition. Holden asks about his date with Jane, and when Stradlater indicates that he might have had sex with her, Holden becomes enraged and tries to punch Stradlater, who quickly overpowers him and knocks him out. Soon after, Holden decides to leave Pencey that night and not to wait until Wednesday. He leaves Pencey to return to New York City, where he will stay in a hotel before actually going home.

On the train to New York, Holden sits next to the mother of a Pencey student, Ernest Morrow. Claiming that his name is actually Rudolf Schmidt (the name of the Pencey janitor), Holden lies to Mrs. Morrow about how popular and well-respected her son is at Pencey— actually Ernest is loathed by the other boys. Holden invites her to have a drink with him at the club car. When Holden reaches New York, he does not know whom he should call. He considers inviting his younger sister, Phoebe, as well as Jane Gallagher and another friend, Sally Hayes. He finally decides to stay at the Edmond Hotel.

From his window he can see other guests at the hotel, including a transvestite and a couple who spit drinks back at each other, which makes him think about sex. He decides to call Faith Cavendish, a former burlesque stripper and reputed prostitute, but she rejects his advances. He thus goes down to the Lavender Room, a nightclub in the Hotel, where he dances with Bernice Krebs, a blonde woman from Seattle who is vacationing in New York with several friends. Holden thinks that these tourists seem pathetic because of their excitement over the various sights of the city.

After leaving the Lavender Room, Holden decides to go to Ernie's, a nightclub in Greenwich Village that his brother D.B. would often frequent before he moved to Hollywood. He leaves almost immediately after he arrives, because he sees Lillian Simmons, one of D.B.'s former girlfriends, and wishes to avoid her because she is a "phony." He walks back to the hotel, where Maurice, the elevator man, offers him a prostitute for the night. He accepts. When Sunny, the prostitute, arrives, Holden becomes too nervous and refuses to go on with it. She demands ten dollars anyway, but Holden believes that he only owes five based on the earlier deal. Sunny and Maurice soon return, however, and demand the extra five dollars. Holden argues with them, but Maurice threatens him while Sunny steals the money. Maurice punches him in the stomach before leaving. Holden then imagines shooting Maurice in the stomach and even jumping out of the window to commit suicide.

Holden calls Sally Hayes to meet her for a matinee. He leaves his bags at a locker at Grand Central Station so that he will not have to go back to the hotel, where he might again face Maurice. At Grand Central Station he talks with two nuns about Romeo and Juliet and insists on giving them a donation. He shops for a record for Phoebe and feels depressed when he hears children singing the song, "If a body catch a body coming through the rye." He meets Sally, and he immediately wants to marry her, even though he does not particularly like her.

They go to see a show starring the Lunts, which he knows Sally will enjoy because it seems sophisticated. After the show, Sally keeps mentioning that she sees a boy from Andover whom she knows, and Holden responds by telling her to go over and give the boy "a big soul kiss." While she talks to the boy, Holden becomes disgusted at how phony the conversation is. Holden and Sally go ice skating and then have lunch together. During lunch, Holden complains that he is fed up with everything around him and suggests that they run away together to New England, where they can live in a cabin in the woods. When she dismisses the idea, Holden calls her a "royal pain in the ass," causing her to cry.

After the date, Holden calls Carl Luce, a friend from the Whooton School who goes to Columbia, and meets him at the Wicker Bar. Carl soon becomes annoyed at Holden for having a "typical Caulfield conversation"—one that is preoccupied with sex—and he suggests that Holden see a psychiatrist. Holden remains at the Wicker Bar, where he gets drunk, then leaves to wander around Central Park. He nearly breaks down when he breaks Phoebe's record. He thinks he may die of pneumonia.

Thinking that he may die soon, Holden returns home to see Phoebe, attempting to avoid his parents. He awakens her, but she soon becomes distressed when she hears that Holden has failed out of Pencey. She says that their father will kill him. He tells her that he might go out to a ranch in Colorado, but she dismisses his idea as foolish.

When he complains about the phoniness of Pencey, Phoebe asks him if he actually likes anything. He claims that he likes Allie, and he thinks about how he likes the nuns at Grand Central and a boy at Elkton Hills who committed suicide. He tells Phoebe that he would like to be "a catcher in the rye," and he imagines himself standing at the edge of a cliff as children play around him. He would come out of somewhere and always catch them just before they fell off the edge.

When his parents come home, Holden sneaks out to stay with Mr. Antolini, his former English teacher at Elkton Hills. Mr. Antolini tells Holden that he is headed for a serious fall and that he is the type who may die nobly for a highly unworthy cause. He quotes Wilhelm Stekel: "The mark of an immature man is that he wants to die nobly for a cause, while the mark of the mature man is that he wants to live humbly for one." Holden falls asleep on the couch. When he awakens, he finds Mr. Antolini with his hand on Holden's head. Holden immediately interprets this as a homosexual advance, so he decides to leave. He tells Mr. Antolini that he has to get his bags from Grand Central Station but will return soon.

In fact, however, Holden spends the night at Grand Central Station, then sends a note to Phoebe at school, telling her to meet him for lunch. He becomes increasingly distraught and delusional, believing that he will die every time he crosses the street. He falls unconscious after suffering from diarrhea. When he meets Phoebe, she tells him that she wants to go with him and becomes angry when he refuses. He buys Phoebe a ticket for the carousel at the nearby zoo, and as he watches her, he begins to cry.

Holden ends his story here. He refuses to relate what happened next and how he got sick. He notes that people are concerned about whether or not he will apply himself next year. He ends the story by relating that he misses Stradlater and Ackley and even Maurice.

Quotes and Analysis

In my mind, I'm probably the biggest sex maniac you ever saw.

Holden Caulfield

One of Holden's greatest internal quandaries regards how to resolve the paradox of love and sex. Holden wants to feel the deepest type of love possible, the love that died when he lost his sibling years ago. The intensity of his raging adolescent hormones makes him think that somehow sex would be joined with that same depth of love for a another person, though in reality sex comes all too easily with money rather than authentic feeling. In his mind, Holden suggests, he is fantasizing constantly about sex, and his friend suggests that the "typical Caulfield conversation" is preoccupied with sex. Yet, the reality is that he never brings this mania into practice; sex without love can be at best a temporary release of the pain of loneliness.

I was half in love with her by the time we sat down. That's the thing about girls. Every time they do something pretty, even if they're not much to look at, or even if they're sort of stupid, you fall half in love with them, and then you never know where the hell you are. Girls. Jesus Christ. They can drive you crazy. They really can.

Holden Caulfield

Here, Holden reflects on the adolescent male's (or perhaps most males', most people's) tendency to overreach, to create relationships in their minds on the basis of a single seemingly genuine encounter. A single "pretty" thing launches fantasies of love. The more alienated and lonely Holden becomes, the more he recedes into his own fantasies, yet he recognizes that seeking pleasure through this kind of imagination is just "crazy," not an authentic way to temper the pain he feels.

People never notice anything.

Holden Caulfield

Many of the most famous lines in Salinger's novel begin with the word "People." For Holden, the word marks Holden's attempt to separate himself from others. Holden is not like other "people"; the world is against him. Generalizing in this way, setting himself apart, can make him feel better about his own idiosyncrasies and low self-esteem, giving him a sense that he is better than the mass of people, who fail to notice what he perceives. Holden sees through phoniness while others accept it.

What I was really hanging around for, I was trying to feel some kind of a good-by. I mean I've left schools and places I didn't even know I was leaving them. I hate that. I don't care if it's a sad good-by or a bad good-by, but when I leave a place I like to know I'm leaving it. If you don't, you feel even worse.

Holden Caulfield

On one level, this is about what is called "closure," the sense that a chapter of his life has ended, with a certain level of consent to leaving a place, letting it go. Sometimes, it seems, a suspension led to an expulsion before Holden had a chance for closure. At a deeper level, however, Holden realizes in this case that he has trouble getting to that feeling of closure; he has a hard time with feelings anymore. Hanging around, he is hoping to get to the feeling of goodbye. When he leaves Pencey, he wants to at least feel a sense of vindication, triumph, or at least sadness or regret. He seems to feel little or nothing, however, reinforcing how disconnected he feels from himself. More broadly, his entire journey is an attempt to reconnect with feelings and emotions long buried, to get all the goodbyes out of the way and clear his troubles so that he can finally move on after Allie's death.

When I really worry about something, I don't just fool around. I even have to go to the bathroom when I worry about something. Only, I don't go. I'm too worried to go. I don't want to interrupt my worrying to go.

Holden Caulfield

Holden appears to have a rich mental life, but it often debilitates him. He does not worry like the phonies, he feels; for him, the worry is all-consuming. Worry, however, is about something other than the present reality; for him it seems to be involved with the neuroses and fantasies which plague him and lead him in search of some greater fulfillment in life. All the worrying seems to be a defense against the pain of reality.

Goddam money. It always ends up making you blue as hell.

Holden Caulfield

Holden picks up on the usual critique of consumerism and greed: money corrupts and does not in itself buy happiness. His own experience shows that he has not spent his money on things that have brought relief of his pain, and whatever hope he had at the time of spending is dashed in the realization that it has not made him feel better. There is also a subtext in his statement: Holden apparently is from a wealthy family that can afford to send him to private schools, which has alienated him.

Anyway, I keep picturing all these little kids playing some game in this big field of rye and all. Thousands of little kids, and nobody's around - nobody big, I mean - except me. And I'm standing on the edge of some crazy cliff. What I have to do, I have to catch everybody if they start to go over the cliff - I mean if they're running and they don't look where they're going I have to come out from somewhere and catch them. That's all I do all day. I'd just be the catcher in the rye and all. I know it's crazy, but that's the only thing I'd really like to be.

Holden Caulfield

This is probably the most famous passage in Salinger's novel, being the source of its title. It attests to Holden's desire to play the rescuer to all the children who might suffer in their lives. They can continue along in their innocence doing what they like, and Holden will be there to make sure that the one deadly boundary is not crossed. They do not need to look where they are going during their game so long as there is someone to catch them at the edge. Moreover, they do not know he is there to watch over them, godlike, unless they really need his help at the last moment. This is Holden's fantasy because a catcher would have caught Allie or, failing that, would have caught Holden and saved him from his descent into loneliness and pain.

Don't ever tell anybody anything. If you do, you start missing everybody.

Holden Caulfield

Holden lives in such pain, having given himself to his brother and then watched him die, that he cannot bear to open up to anyone again because of the thought of loss, having to lose something that meant everything. Here, telling someone something means opening up to say something authentic. This is not something he would advise, however, because the closeness and trust involved in this genuine act not only will one day be lost, but also will show that one does not have this closeness or trust with others.

It's no fun to be yellow. Maybe I'm not all yellow. I don't know. I think maybe I'm just partly yellow and partly the type that doesn't give much of a damn if they lose their gloves.

Holden Caulfield

Here Holden acknowledges some of his cowardice. He is not the kind of weenie who worries over lost gloves; no, when he worries, he worries about deep issues and puts his whole self into it. Maybe that is genuine worry, he thinks, rather than "yellow" fear of the kind felt by the phonies in the world.

I don't even know what I was running for--I guess I just felt like it.

Holden Caulfield

This is a telling statement about Holden's orientation toward his present life. He is running from his feelings, often not for any conscious reason but to avoid what may happen if he stops long enough to examine them. When he is choosing to avoid authentic human interaction in order to avoid the future pain of loss, it is more of an emotional choice than a rational comparison of one pain against another.

Summary and Analysis of Chapters 1-2

Chapter 1

The Catcher in the Rye begins with a statement by the narrator, Holden Caulfield, that he will not recount his "lousy" childhood and "all that David Copperfield kind of crap" because such details bore him. He describes his parents as nice but "touchy as hell." Instead, Holden vows to relate what happened to him around last Christmas, before he had to take it easy. He also mentions his brother, D.B., who is nearby in Hollywood "being a prostitute." Holden was a student at Pencey Prep in Agerstown, Pennsylvania, and he mocks their advertisements, which claim to have been molding boys into clear-thinking young men since 1888.

Holden begins his story during the Saturday of the football game with Saxon Hall, which is supposed to be a big deal at Pencey. Selma Thurmer, the daughter of the headmaster, is at the game, but Holden is not. Although she is unattractive and a bit pathetic, to Holden she seems nice enough because she avoids lavishing praise upon her father. Holden, the manager of the fencing team, has just returned from New York with the team. Although they were supposed to have a meet with the McBurney School, Holden left the foils on the subway. The fencing team became furious with Holden, but he cannot help but find humor in the bad situation. Holden has not gone to the game as a result of his sudden unpopularity. Instead he chooses to say goodbye to Spencer, his history teacher, who knows that Holden is not coming back to Pencey. It turns out that Holden has recently been expelled for failing four classes.

Chapter Two

Holden finds Spencer's house somewhat depressing, smelling of Vicks Nose Drops and clearly underscoring the old age of its inhabitants. Mr. Spencer sits in a ratty old bathrobe and asks Holden to sit down. Holden tells him that Dr. Thurmer lectured him about how "life is a game" and that one should "play it according to the rules"—just before he expelled him. Mr. Spencer replies that Dr. Thurmer was correct, but Holden holds to the thought that life is only a game if you are on the right side.

Holden tells Mr. Spencer that his parents will be upset, for this is his fourth private school so far. Holden recounts that, at sixteen, he is over six feet tall and has some gray hair, but still acts like a child, as others often tell him. Spencer says that he met with Holden's parents, who are "grand" people, but Holden dismisses that word as "phony." Spencer then tells Holden that he failed him in History because he knew nothing. Spencer reads him his exam essay about the Egyptians, which is woefully inadequate. At the end of the exam, Holden left a note for Mr. Spencer admitting that he was not interested in the Egyptians despite Spencer's interesting lectures, noting that he would accept if Mr. Spencer failed him.

As Holden and Mr. Spencer continue to talk, Holden's mind wanders to the ducks in Central Park. He wonders how they suddenly vanish in the winter and where they go. When Spencer asks why Holden quit Elkton Hills, he replies that it is a long story. In short, the people there were phonies. He mentions the particular quality of the headmaster, Mr. Haas, who would be charming toward everyone except the "funny-looking parents." Holden claims he has little interest in the future, and he assures Spencer that he is just going through a phase. As Holden leaves, he hears Spencer say "good luck," a phrase that he particularly loathes.

Analysis

In Chapter 1, J.D. Salinger has his protagonist begin *The Catcher in the Rye* with a bold and sarcastic declaration. Holden immediately rejects the idea that the events that he describes in the novel consist of his life story or that this story is indicative of any larger message. He eschews the Dickensian idea of literature in novels like *David Copperfield*, in which the plot and narrative progress with a moral message, and he does not intend to inspire sympathy for himself like another David Copperfield or Oliver Twist. Besides, he is probably at a boarding school because his parents are wealthy. Instead of pointing toward a moral, he adopts a discursive style with no concrete message. His story is what it is, and Holden's story is his own, not really a cautionary tale for others. As Holden insists, his tale exists independent of any larger meaning or message.

Nevertheless, a reader might pick up on Salinger's use of the conventions of a cautionary tale; there is something human about his experience that may well teach us something about not living badly. Holden indicates that he has to "take it easy" at a new place, strongly implying that he now is receiving psychiatric or psychological help. The details in the first chapter already indicate that he has pursued an aimless, self-destructive path. Expelled from school for failing several classes, Holden essentially describes himself as a perpetual failure. Even worse, in his failings he appears to have a strong disregard for others. His solipsistic self-destruction makes him unable to grasp the consequences of his actions, such as when he chooses humor and argues that he somehow is not responsible after he loses the fencing equipment on the trip to New York.

Holden is in many ways a typical teenager, skeptical of all authority and having a truculent attitude that stems from cynicism and naïveté. Within the first several paragraphs he dismisses his parents as "touchy" and his brother as a sellout to Hollywood consumerism, yet he provides no good examples of their behavior. With the exception of Mr. Spencer and, to some degree, Selma Thurmer, Holden displays contempt for every character he mentions and the actions they undertake. The one value that he tends to espouse is authenticity, but he has no concrete definition of what this entails. Although he disdains Selma Thurmer's failed attempts to artificially improve her appearance, his greatest compliment about the headmaster's daughter is that she portrays her father honestly. This focus on authenticity and, in turn, the essential phoniness of others around him, will be a recurring theme for

Holden Caulfield.

At this point, the major literary devices to take note of are a strong point of view, anchored in the first-person narrator, as well as a clear sense of the novel's themes. The tone of the novel is also interesting to explore because Holden dominates the narrative so overtly. While Holden's tone is sarcastic and mocking, the tone of the novel seems more melancholy; we can already sense our antihero's loneliness and pain.

In Chapter 2, Salinger continues to develop the history of Holden Caulfield. It is not his full life story, but this recent history is perhaps the most telling part of his life so far. Salinger gradually indicates that Caulfield has a longer history and troubles that are more deeply rooted than those of the conventional disaffected teenager; Holden moves from boarding school to boarding school with no sense of purpose. Even Holden's style of narration reveals his lack of a coherent vision. He admits that he cannot concentrate on any particular topic, thinking about ice skating while Mr. Spencer lectures him.

As established in the previous chapter, Holden exemplifies the typical teenage feeling of alienation. He rejects the idea that life is a game, convinced that he is a misunderstood underdog (despite being a teenager privileged enough to move easily among Eastern prep schools), and he justifies his immaturity by claiming that he is going through a phase. His critiques are glib and without much substance, such as his insistence that others are "phonies" and his dislike of certain phrases such as "good luck." He may be right in his critique, realizing that social relations and language are very often inauthentic, but his level of alienation has been taken to the extreme of making him unfit for regular human society. Holden's diatribes against phonies are particularly instructive, but he does not always practice what he preaches; although he insists upon authenticity, he humors and flatters Mr. Spencer by agreeing with him.

Holden, then, demonstrates a great aversion for everything associated with adulthood, such as the smell of Vicks Nose Drops that permeates Mr. Spencer's home and the behavior of Mr. Haas, just as he occupies a precarious space between childhood and the adult world. In appearance he is an adult, with his tall stature and prematurely graying hair, yet as he and others around him realize, he is still quite immature.

Holden's behavior is not typical and excusable adolescent behavior, and Mr. Spencer shatters his ideal of authenticity by dismissing Holden's vague justifications for his behavior and by confronting him with his failures. Holden's desire to be authentic looks more like solipsism, a critique to which Holden cannot respond. But what if Holden is just taking a good idea to a bad extreme? Is it not true that maturity entails not just a loss of innocence but also a certain capitulation to phoniness? Holden is resisting the idea that in order to have the life he might want, he might have to satisfy others' ideas about what is good. If we do what others want instead of what we would prefer to do, yes, it is a kind of phoniness, yet we might better call it humility, service, or learning from others.

Summary and Analysis of Chapters 3-5

Chapter 3

Holden claims that he is the most terrific liar one could ever meet. He admits that he lied to Spencer by telling him that he had to go to the gym. At Pencey, Holden lives in the Ossenburger Memorial Wing of the new dorms. Ossenburger, a wealthy undertaker, graduated from the school, and Holden relates how "phony" Ossenburger seemed when he gave a speech exalting faith in Jesus. Holden returns to his room, where he puts on a red hunting hat he bought in New York. He thinks about the books that he likes to read—he prefers Ring Lardner, but he is now reading Dinesen's *Out of Africa*.

Ackley, a student whose room is connected to Holden's, barges in. Ackley has a terrible personality and an even worse complexion. Holden tries to ignore him, then pretends that he is blind. Ackley cuts his nails right in front of Holden. Ackley claims that he hates Ward Stradlater, Holden's roommate, as a "goddamn sonuvabitch," but Holden tells Ackley that the real reason is that Stradlater told him that he should actually brush his teeth. Holden further defends Stradlater, claiming that he is conceited but generous.

Stradlater arrives and is friendly to Holden. He asks Holden if he may borrow a jacket from him. Stradlater walks around shirtless to show off his build.

Chapter 4

Since he has nothing else to do, Holden goes down to the bathroom to chat with Stradlater as he shaves. Stradlater, in comparison to Ackley, is a "secret" slob, who would always shave with a rusty razor that he would never clean. Stradlater is a "Yearbook" kind of handsome guy. He asks Holden to write a composition for him for English. Holden realizes the irony that he is flunking out of Pencey, yet is still asked to do work for others. Stradlater insists, however, that Holden not write it too well, for the teacher knows that Holden is a hot-shot in English.

On an impulse, Holden gives Stradlater a half nelson, which greatly annoys Stradlater. Stradlater talks about his date that night with Jane Gallagher. Although Stradlater cannot even get her name correct, Holden knows her well, for she lived next door to him several summers ago and they would play checkers together. Stradlater barely listens as he fixes his hair with Holden's gel. Holden asks Stradlater not to tell Jane that he got kicked out. He then borrows Holden's hound's-tooth jacket and leaves. Ackley returns, and Holden is actually glad to see him, for he takes his mind off of Jane Gallagher.

Chapter 5

On Saturday nights at Pencey, the students are served steak. Holden believes this occurs because parents visit on Sunday and students can thus tell them that they had steak for dinner the previous night, as if it were a common occurrence. Holden goes with Ackley and Mal Brossard into New York City to see a movie, but since Ackley and Brossard had both seen that particular Cary Grant comedy, they play pinball and get hamburgers instead.

When they return, Ackley remains in Holden's room, telling them about a girl he had sex with, but Holden knows that he is lying, for whenever he tells that same story, the details always change. Holden tells him to leave so that he can write Stradlater's composition. He writes about his brother Allie's baseball mitt. Allie, born two years after Holden, died of leukemia in 1946. The night that Allie died, Holden broke all of the windows in his garage with his fist.

Analysis

In Chapter 3, Holden's admission that he is the "most terrific liar" one could meet is interesting given his detestation of phoniness. It is an apt self-identification, for his delusions are not so much about making others believe his deceptions (it is doubtful that persons such as Mr. Spencer believe Holden's lies) but about self-delusion. Continuing to berate others for phoniness, Holden cannot recognize his considerable failings. He claims to be both illiterate and an avid reader, but when identifying his favorite authors he cannot identify any particular reason why he likes their works. In addition, as we perceive later, Holden lies to himself about shutting himself off from the deep emotion of love, since he clearly wants to love another despite his idea that he never wants to take the risk again after his brother's death.

Salinger introduces two other Pencey students in this chapter, each of whom represent contrasting types of reprehensible behavior. Ackley is ostentatiously boorish; in appearance and in manners he is disgusting and oblivious to all social graces. Hopelessly vulgar and unclean, Ackley is unaware of the contempt that Holden Caulfield has for him, even when Holden confronts him with it. Stradlater, in contrast, is outwardly friendly and considerate, yet still one of the phonies that Holden abhors. Stradlater is playful and charming, but is still self-centered and arrogant. He flaunts his assets, whether physical or monetary. Whether giving away a tie or strutting around the dormitory in a state of undress, he performs these actions to show what he possesses. These characters do, nevertheless, serve the purpose of showing the stifling conditions that Holden faces at Pencey. Ackley and Stradlater demonstrate that Holden's disgust for the school and its "phonies" is not completely unfounded. Both characters, then, serve as 'foils' to Holden -- illuminating both his strengths and weaknesses as the protagonist.

However, Holden's descriptions of both of these characters cannot be trusted entirely. Overall, Holden is an unreliable narrator whose conceptions of the characters reveal his particular point of view. These descriptions must be taken with some skepticism, for they reveal Holden's skewed perspective on others. This also can be seen in Holden's description of Ossenburger. Holden can view his contribution to the school only in cynical terms: He thinks that Ossenburger prays to Jesus "to send him a few more stiffs." Holden is inherently suspicious of all around him, particularly authority figures. His view that adults serve only their self-interest is aggressively cynical, and his disillusionment with reality has crystallized into a jaded naïveté.

Salinger devotes Chapter 4 to Holden's fixation on Stradlater's behavior. Holden has an eye for detail and the nuances of Stradlater's behavior; he even analyzes the rhythm of the conversation that the two have when Stradlater asks Holden to write a paper for him. Stradlater emerges as conceited and self-centered and obsessed with his appearance and image. Although Holden does not employ his standard term "phony" to describe Stradlater in this chapter, he makes it clear that Stradlater exemplifies a strong sense of artificiality.

According to Holden, Stradlater is "Yearbook" handsome, implying that his attractive appearance is best shown in photographs and is thus divorced from Stradlater's actual self. Salinger also makes the distinction between appearances and actuality when Holden describes Stradlater's dirty razor, which demonstrates that Stradlater is only concerned with matters that relate to his public persona. Stradlater compounds his vanity with a strong egotism. He cannot even remember the name of his date that evening, and expects Holden to write his paper for him simply because he asked.

However, if Stradlater is vapid and superficial, Holden proves himself equally so by detailing each of these aspects of his roommate's behavior with such precision. Holden does not let any slight against him go unnoticed, such as Stradlater's use of his jacket and his hair gel. Like Stradlater, Holden has a narrow focus; however, his self-centered behavior does not center on physical appearance as it does with Stradlater. Both use others as means to a particular end. Stradlater uses Holden for favors such as writing papers, while Holden uses Ackley for amusement.

Stradlater does, however, give the reader a new perspective on Holden Caulfield. Holden does have his merits, as Stradlater indicates when he asks him to write his composition. Beneath the cynical self-absorption, Holden may be a talented and intelligent writer who fails to apply himself to tasks. Holden continues to behave erratically throughout the chapter. He does things purely out of impulse, such as giving Stradlater a half-nelson. This pattern of behavior will continue throughout the novel on a larger, more destructive scale.

Salinger foreshadows the source of Holden Caulfield's psychological troubles in Chapter 5 when he describes the composition that Holden writes for Stradlater. Holden elaborates on his family history, recounting how his brother Allie died of leukemia. This may be one of the events that has caused Holden's current psychological troubles, although as narrator Holden seems to resist such simplistic interpretations. Whatever the cause of his difficulties, the paper does reveal that

Allie's death is still a major concern for Holden and that the erratic and often violent behavior that Holden demonstrates during the course of his tale has a precedent.

As we continue, we'll look specifically for the subtext of how Allie's death perhaps precipitated this deep alienation in Holden and caused him to lose himself to cynicism and repressed pain. All in all, The Catcher in the Rye is the story of a boy who once loved something so much that he cannot dare to love again now that the person is gone. The theme of 'pain avoidance,' then, however mundane, becomes the secret to decoding all of Holden's self-destructive behavior. In order to heal, he will have to learn to love again without fear and without shutting down.

Summary and Analysis of Chapters 6-10

Chapter 6

Stradlater returns late that night, thanks Holden for the jacket and asks if he wrote the composition for him. When Stradlater reads it, he gets upset at Holden, because it is simply about a baseball glove. Irritated that Stradlater is upset, Holden tears up the composition. Immediately Holden starts smoking, just to further annoy Stradlater.

Holden asks about the date, but Stradlater doesn't give much information, only that they spent most of the time in Ed Banky's car. Finally Holden asks if Stradlater "gave her the time," a crude way of asking if they had sex. Stradlater says that the answer is a "professional secret," and Holden furiously responds by trying to punch him.

Stradlater pushes him down and sits with his knees on Holden's chest. He only lets Holden go when he agrees to say nothing more about Stradlater's date. But when Holden calls Stradlater a moron, Stradlater knocks him out. At Stradlater's command, Holden then goes to the bathroom to wash the blood off his face. Even though he claims to be a pacifist, Holden enjoys the look of blood on his face.

Chapter 7

Ackley, who was awakened by the fight, comes in Holden's room to ask what happened. He tells Holden that he is still bleeding and should put something on his wounds. Holden asks if he can sleep in Ackley's room that night, since his roommate is away for the weekend, but Ackley says that he can't give him permission. Holden feels so lonesome that he wishes he were dead.

Holden worries that Stradlater had sex with Jane during their date, because he knew that Stradlater was capable of seducing girls quickly. Holden asks Ackley whether or not one has to be Catholic to join a monastery. He then decides to leave Pencey immediately. He decides to take a room in a hotel in New York and take it easy until Wednesday. He packs ice skates that his mother had just sent him. The skates make him sad, because they were not the kind that he wanted. According to Holden, his mother has a way of somehow disappointing him whenever he receives a present.

Holden wakes up Woodruff, a wealthy student, and sells him his typewriter for twenty bucks. Before he leaves, he yells into the halls of Pencey, "Sleep tight, ya morons!"

Chapter 8

Since it is too late to call a cab, Holden walks to the train station. On the train, a woman gets on at Trenton and sits right beside him, even though the train is nearly empty. She strikes up a conversation with him, noticing the Pencey sticker on his suitcase, and says that her son, Ernest Morrow, goes to Pencey as well. Holden remembers him as "the biggest bastard that ever went to Pencey." Holden tells her that his name is Rudolf Schmidt, the name of the Pencey janitor. Holden lies to Mrs. Morrow, pretending that he likes Pencey and that he is good friends with Ernest.

Mrs. Morrow, meanwhile, thinks that her son is 'sensitive,' an term that Holden finds laughable, but Holden continues to tell lies about Ernest - including that her son would have been elected class president, but he was too modest to accept the nomination. Holden then asks if she would like to join him for a cocktail in the club car. Finally, he tells her that he is leaving Pencey early because he has to have an operation; he claims he has a tumor in his brain. When she invites Holden to visit during the summer, he says that he will be spending the summer in South America with his grandmother.

Chapter 9

When Holden reaches New York, he does not know whom to call. He considers calling his kid sister, Phoebe, but she would be asleep and his parents would overhear. He also considers calling Jane Gallagher or Sally Hayes, another female friend, but ultimately does not call anybody.

He gets into a cab and absentmindedly gives the driver his home address, but soon realizes that he does not want to get home. He goes to the Edmond Hotel instead, where he stays in a shabby room. He looks out of the window and can see the other side of the hotel. From this view he can see other rooms; in one of them, a man takes off his clothes and puts on ladies' clothing, while in another a man and a woman spit their drinks at one another.

Holden thinks that he himself is the "biggest sex maniac you ever saw," but then paradoxically claims that he does not understand sex at all. He then thinks of calling Jane Gallagher but again decides against it, and instead considers calling a woman named Faith Cavendish, who was formerly a burlesque stripper and is not quite a prostitute. When he calls her, he continues to ask whether or not they might get a drink together, but she turns him down at every opportunity.

Chapter 10

Holden describes his family in more detail in the course of this chapter. His sister Phoebe is the smartest little kid that he has ever met, and Holden himself is the only dumb one. Phoebe reminds Holden of Allie in physical appearance, but she is very emotional. She writes books about imaginary Hazle Weatherfield, a girl detective.

Holden goes down to the Lavender Room, a nightclub in the hotel. The band there is putrid and the people are mostly old. When he attempts to order a drink, the waiter asks for identification, but since he does not have proof of his age, he begs the waiter to put rum in his Coke.

Holden "gives the eye" to three women at another table, in particular a blonde one. He asks the blonde one to dance, and Holden judges her to be an excellent dancer, but a moron. Holden is offended when the woman, Bernice Krebs, asks his age, but he tells these women, who are visiting from Seattle, that his name is Jim Steele. Since they keep mentioning how they saw Peter Lorre that day, Holden claims that he just saw Gary Cooper, who just left the Lavender Room. Holden thinks that the women are sad for wanting to go to the first show at Radio City Music Hall.

Analysis

By Chapter 6, Salinger has established that Holden suffers some great psychological difficulties, yet knowledge of these instances come from secondary sources. But in this chapter, Salinger brings Holden's unpredictable behavior clearly to the fore. Holden behaves almost solely on impulse, even when there seems to be no rational motivation for his behavior.

As this chapter demonstrates, this inability to control his behavior reaches far beyond any normal teenage impulses, as shown when Holden rips up Stradlater's essay when he fails to appreciate Holden's work. The fight between Stradlater and Holden also shows Holden's inability to control himself; when he suspects that Stradlater has slept with his old friend, Holden responds by punching him.

This event reveals contradictory impulses within Holden. Although he claims that he is a pacifist, a dubious statement that reinforces his status as an unreliable narrator, Holden seems disconnected from the violence he causes and the pain that he suffers. He views his fight from a distant perspective, appreciating the look of his bloody face without considering the actual fight itself. This predilection for extreme behavior and lack of connection to his own actions will be a consistent theme throughout The Catcher in the Rye, as Holden continues to allow his behavior to reach disturbing extremes. Indeed, The Catcher in the Rye, for all its apparent episodic nature and aimlessness, actually follows a pretty traditional structure, complete with intensifying rising action, leading to a climax, and then ultimately a denouement.

In Chapter 7, Despite the fact that Holden is still bleeding from his fight with Stradlater, he remains curiously unconcerned with his wounds, allowing his mind to focus upon details external to his action physical condition. Holden reveals more of his psychology during this chapter. His greatest concern seems to be whether Stradlater seduced Jane Gallagher, revealing an unhealthy, if predictable, view on sexuality.

Holden follows his thoughts on Jane Gallagher by musing about joining a monastery and thus becoming celibate. Holden seems to harbor a disgust for any type of sexuality, whether Ackley's obviously false boasts or Stradlater's successful seductions. At this point Salinger leaves ambiguous the actual reason why Holden would be concerned about Jane Gallagher in particular, for the only information

Holden gives about Jane is that they would often play checkers together.

Holden finally reaches a breaking point in this chapter by leaving Pencey early, with no concrete plan for what he will do. In many ways this is typical of Holden's established patterns of behavior: impulsive, selfish and aimless. His final insult to his fellow students shows that Holden believes himself to be in some major respect different from the other Pencey students, possessing a greater, more acute intelligence.

An innate sense of superiority, however unfounded, separates Holden from the other students, for he believes himself to be more honorable and 'deep' than the vapid and self-centered Stradlater and more refined than the piggish Ackley. Yet Holden demonstrates qualities similar to those of his peers; he suffers from a self-imposed delusion that he is different and misunderstood and chooses to leave Pencey for an uncertain future. At this point, then, we're not quite sure whether Holden is a protagonist or antagonist in terms of how we should relate to him. Perhaps the better term for him is 'anti-hero,' meaning we sympathize with him because of his failures as a protagonist.

Setting is also crucial here as we see Holden move from the world of his boarding school out into the real world. In his mind, it is the priggish and boorish world of the school that is holding him back from truly being a fulfilled and happy person. Now as we move out into the real world, we'll begin to get a sense of whether Holden can get past his own walls in order to grow and access his feelings. Indeed, the book seems to hit a key crossroads here -- is the book a 'critical mimesis of bourgeois life in the Eastern United States,' as some critics call it? (Salzman 2). Or is the book an exploration of Holden's own hypocrisy?

In Chapter 8, Holden bolsters his earlier claim that he is an excellent liar, as his conversation with Mrs. Morrow contains nothing but falsehoods. The only statement that he makes to Mrs. Morrow that contains any truth is that he is a student at Pencey; otherwise, all of his statements are deliberately misleading. He tells Mrs. Morrow exactly what she wants to hear about her son, humoring her own sense of vanity and self-absorption by making her believe that her son, whom Holden loathes, is one of the most honorable and decent students at Pencey. These lies reveal the complete contempt that Holden holds for Mrs. Morrow and, by extension, all authority figures. He lies in order to mock Mrs. Morrow's sense of delusion while relishing the false view that she has of her son. Holden claims a sense of superiority over Mrs. Morrow, for he believes that he can see clearly Ernest Morrow's personality, while she has a false, idealized portrait of her son. Whatever her delusions, however, Holden treats Mrs. Morrow horribly. He views her either as a target for ridicule or a sexual object, as he flirts with her and even offers to buy her a drink.

This chapter is indicative of Holden's state of mind. He takes a trait that demonstrates a typical teenage immaturity, in this case lying and flatter adults, and moves it to an unbearable extreme; his lies become more shameless and outlandish, revealing the disturbing disconnect between Holden's psyche and reality.

In the first part of Chapter 9, Salinger demonstrates that Holden has absolutely no purpose for his actions. He wavers between decisions, whether the decision involves whom he should call when he arrives or where he should go. Holden approaches these decisions haphazardly, almost reaching his home address before realizing that he wants to avoid his parents.

His decision-making process, however, does reveal Holden's particular preoccupations. He has a fixation with Jane Gallagher that reaches beyond what the original mentions of her would indicate. When he thinks of Jane Gallagher, his mind wanders to sexual matters, but he does not think of sex related directly to her. This indicates that Holden suffers from a Madonna/whore complex; he can view a woman either in terms of absolute purity or absolute degradation but cannot reconcile this view. Holden even explicitly conceives of sex in disgusting terms. When he muses on sexual matters, he repeatedly describes such behavior as "crumby," but then admits that he himself is "pretty horny" and cannot control the sexual urges that can "spoil anything really good."

Salinger further demonstrates Holden's Madonna/whore complex through the juxtaposition of Jane Gallagher and Faith Cavendish, who represent two opposing aspects of female sexuality. To Holden, Jane Gallagher is the prototypical 'good' girl whom he remembers for playing checkers, while Faith Cavendish is nothing more than a prostitute. Both women, then, are symbols of Holden's increasing alienation from society.

By Chapter 10, we can analyze the tone of Salinger's novel in the context of Holden's narration to discover, as Walcutt has it, that

> The most obvious way to account for the tone and flavor [of the book] is to assume that the hero is telling the story to an analyst or a doctor. It is familiar, even intimate, defensive, bragging, and yet also expostulatory, if not apologetic. (317)

Indeed, there's a showboat quality to Holden's narration at the beginning - this need to impress his audience - which gradually breaks down over the course of the novel as he becomes increasingly vulnerable and scared. Soon, instead of treating his audience as spectators to be entertained and impressed, he begins to treat us as therapists -- even priests to confess to.

Moreover, Salinger continues to establish Holden as a character with an entirely cynical view of others around him, particularly women and even including himself. His cynicism reaches nearly all those with whom he interacts, with a few notable exceptions. The most significant exception to emerge in this chapter is Phoebe, Holden's young sister. He lavishes nearly unconditional praise on Phoebe, detailing without any apparent sense of irony her intelligence and talents.

He even appears charmed by her foibles, such as misspelling the name of her 'girl detective.' Significantly, Holden compares her to Allie, one of the few other characters for whom Holden does not express contempt. These two characters, along with Jane Gallagher, represent for Holden a sense of innocence and childhood. Phoebe is still a child, Allie never had the change to mature, and Jane exists for Holden as an innocent girl playing checkers.

Those characters who represent an adult sensibility serve primarily as targets for Holden's derision. The three women in the Lavender Room are significant examples of this. Holden finds Bernice's insistence on propriety laughable, and dismisses her and her companions' tourist activities. For Holden, their actions are trite and meaningless, yet while they have a purpose and a plan, however simplistic, Holden behaves randomly and without motivation.

This chapter continues a pattern of pseudonyms that Holden adopts for himself. He treats his interaction with others as a performance, refusing to honestly depict himself to those around him. His honesty is entirely internalized; he admits his faults and lies in narration, but cannot do the same with other persons.

Summary and Analysis of Chapters 11-15

Chapter 11

Upon leaving the Lavender Room, Holden begins to think of Jane Gallagher and worries that Stradlater seduced her. Holden met Jane when his mother became irritated that the Gallagher's Doberman pinscher relieved itself on their lawn. Several days later, he introduced himself to her, but it took some time before he could convince her that he didn't care what their dog did. Holden reminisces about Jane's smile, and admits that she is the only person whom he showed Allie's baseball mitt. The one time that he and Jane did anything sexual together was after she had a fight with Mr. Cudahy, her stepfather. Holden suspected that her stepfather had tried to "get wise with" Jane. Despondent by the course of his thoughts, Holden decides to go to Ernie's, a nightclub in Greenwich village that D.B. used to frequent before he went to Hollywood.

Chapter 12

In the cab to Ernie's, Holden chats with Horwitz, the cab driver. He asks what happens to the ducks in Central Park during the winter, but the two get into an argument when Horwitz thinks that Holden's questions are stupid. Ernie's is filled with prep school and college jerks, as Holden calls them. Holden notices a Joe Yale-looking guy with a beautiful girl; he is telling the girl how a guy in his dorm nearly committed suicide.

Suddenly, a former girlfriend of Holden's brother, D.B., recognizes him. The girl, Lillian Simmons, asks about D.B. and introduces Holden to a Navy commander she is dating. Holden notices how she blocks the aisle in the place as she drones on about how handsome Holden has become. Rather than spend time with Lillian Simmons, Holden leaves.

Chapter 13

Holden walks back to his hotel, although it is forty-one blocks away. He considers how he would confront a person who had stolen his gloves. Although he would not do so aggressively, he wishes that he could threaten the person who stole them. Holden finally concludes that he would yell at the thief but not have the courage to hit him.

Holden then reminisces about drinking with Raymond Goldfarb at Whooton. While back at the hotel, Maurice, the elevator man, asks Holden if he is interested in a little tail tonight. He offers Holden prostitute for five dollars. When she arrives, she does not believe that Holden is twenty-two, as he claims. Holden finally tells the prostitute, Sunny, that he just had an operation on his clavichord, as an excuse not to have sex. She is angry, but he still pays her, even though they argue over the price.

He gives her five dollars, although she demands ten.

Chapter 14

After the prostitute leaves, Holden sits in a chair and talks aloud to his brother Allie, which he often does whenever he is depressed. Finally he gets in bed and feels like praying, although he is "sort of an atheist." He claims that he likes Jesus, but the Disciples annoy him. Other than Jesus, the Biblical character he likes best is the lunatic who lived in the tombs and cut himself with stones. Holden tells that his parents disagree on religion and none of his siblings attend church.

Maurice and Sunny the hooker knock on the door, demanding more money. Holden argues with Maurice and threatens to call the cops, but Maurice says that his parents would find out that he spent the night with a whore. As Holden starts to cry, Sunny takes the money from his wallet. Maurice punches him in the stomach before leaving. After Maurice is gone, Holden imagines that he had taken a bullet and would shoot Maurice in the stomach. Holden feels like committing suicide by jumping out the window, but he wouldn't want people looking at his gory body on the sidewalk.

Chapter 15

Holden calls Sally Hayes, who goes to the Mary A. Woodruff School. According to Holden, Sally seems quite intelligent because she knows a good deal about the theater and literature, but is actually quite stupid. He makes a date to meet Sally for a matinee, but she continues to chat with Holden on the phone despite his lack of interest. Holden tells her that his father is a wealthy corporation attorney and his mother has not been healthy since Allie died. At Grand Central Station, where Holden checks in his bags after leaving the hotel, he sees two nuns with cheap suitcases. Holden reminisces about his roommate at Elkton Hills, Dick Slagle who had cheap suitcases and would complain about how everything was bourgeois. He chats with the nuns and gives them a donation.

Analysis

In Chapter 11, Jane Gallagher continues to occupy a great deal of Holden's thoughts, and the stories about her reinforce other themes that emerge throughout The Catcher in the Rye. The story about Jane Gallagher reminds the reader that Allie's death has had a major effect on Holden. For Holden, information about Allie remains secretive and private, to be shared only with certain persons. This also gives more weight to the earlier chapter in which Holden writes a paper about the baseball mitt for Stradlater. This information, which he once considered so private, emerges as part of an essay written for others, indicating that Holden has been repressing certain emotions concerning his brothers death that may eventually emerge.

The chapter also reinforces the recurrent suspicion that Holden has for adults. He believes that Jane Gallagher has been abused by her alcoholic stepfather, which bolsters Holden's idea that all authority figures are dangerous. This also elaborates part of the reason why Holden has such a jaded view of sexuality, for he may associate it with actions such as Mr. Cudahy's predatory behavior toward Jane. Later on, we'll see that Holden himself has suffered at the hands of 'perverts,' as he calls them, when he meets Mr. Antolini. To Holden, then, sex has become something disgusting and not something to celebrate. Instead of relating to love, it's something that is its own decrepit entity, completely closed off from affairs of the heart.

Still, here is a key indication of Holden's hypocrisy and muddled position as a protagonist or antagonist. He seems incapable of the love necessary to reach sexual fulfillment -- and thus seeks sexual satisfaction, which he finds not only morally repugnant, but also deeply unfulfilling.

In Chapter 12, Salinger continues to establish Holden's great dissatisfaction for those around him in this chapter. He continues to show a latent hostility toward everyone he meets, whether Lillian Simmons or Horwitz. In most of these encounters, Holden expresses a false sense of cordiality toward the people he encounters, yet describes only their most negative traits. As he expresses his own false exterior, he becomes fixated on phoniness in others, finding only cynical interpretations of their behavior, such as when he suspects that the "Joe Yale" guy is telling the girl about the suicide attempt while trying to feel her up. What boils up, then, is a primal rage towards others who can find pleasure in the everyday - something Holden is completely incapable of. He is not only dumb, but deep down toxically angry about the impenetrability of his own defenses.

This hostility becomes more pronounced when he argues with Horwitz, who in a minor way challenges Holden for his foolish questions. Holden's anger seems most directed at those of his own particular social situation: he hates "prep school jerks" and "Joe Yale" guys, people who travel in similar circles. This emerges as a particular form of self-loathing. As a prep school student who is expected to attend an Ivy League college, Holden loathes those persons who are most like him. Indeed, he'd rather give himself the name of the Pencey janitor then take responsibility for his own privileged position. He finds romance in pretending to be downtrodden - in feigning oppression.

It might be too facile to say that Holden is simply in the throes of an existential dilemma. He less questions his soul and more holds it in, in order to avoid the pain of living. After Allie's death, it seemed, he was plunged into a true vision of life's suffering, and couldn't bear to stomach it while awash in the trivialities of everyday life. He hates people primarily because they can't see what he does - that life is short and unpredictable, and that love isn't worth giving because it might be taken away.

In Chapter 13, Holden emerges as a scared adolescent in this chapter, as he admits to himself his own cowardice. He believes that he is incapable of standing up to another

Pencey student and fighting him in defense of his property, a claim that stands contradictory to his earlier fight with Stradlater. However, in that instance he fought Stradlater out of sheer impulse. Indeed, if Holden ever fights back, it's never out of a belief that he will vindicate himself, but rather out of a seeming obsession with self-destruction. He wants to be beaten up. He wants to suffer pain. Perhaps it's the only thing that makes him feel alive.

When a decision requires any degree of forethought, moreover, Holden cannot commit to it. This inability to follow through on decisions is also demonstrated during Holden's encounter with the prostitute, which also serves as a reminder of his view of women as either purely virginal or irredeemable whores. The prostitute questions Holden's age, just as others have done during the course of the novel, again proving that however old Holden thinks that he appears, he presents himself as a child to the adult characters around him.

Holden's behavior becomes increasingly self-destructive as Chapter 14 progresses. Although he knows that Maurice and Sunny threaten him, he persists in arguing with them, even though they only dispute a five dollar charge and he believes that he is in serious danger. During this encounter Holden once again reveals himself to be a child, breaking down into tears as soon as Sunny and Maurice take the money from him, yet he displays more than extreme teenage disaffection. Holden fantasizes about murdering Maurice after he leaves, but gives this thought only passing consideration. Rather, the more important threat that Holden poses is to himself. His behavior toward Maurice and Sunny indicates that he is at some level unconcerned that they will hurt him, and he even seems to take some perverse pleasure from the pain Maurice inflicts, as he uses this as a chance for role-playing as a movie gangster.

Salinger includes several instances indicating Holden's masochistic attitudes, such as his admission that his favorite character in the Bible is one who mutilates himself. These details accumulate throughout the chapter to Holden's final revelation that he is considering suicide. Although he finally dismisses the idea of jumping out the window because of the particular details of his death, this is a clear sign of Holden's despair. Salinger clearly foreshadows that Holden will engage in some suicidal action, possibly the reason why he is in psychiatric care as the book begins.

In Chapter 15, after the jarring events of the previous night, Holden returns to his normal state of affairs and preoccupations. He treats Sally Hayes in the same manner as he does the other persons he meets or mentions in the course of the novel: outwardly friendly and cordial while masking a core of contempt for their values and idiosyncrasies. Holden continues to elaborate on his family history, this time expanding the scope of Allie's death to include other family members. Indeed, the death of his brother has had a significant impact on Holden, but has also had devastating consequences for the rest of his family. We sense that the family never recovered and that everyone pulled away from one another, perhaps in self-protection. Only Holden and Phoebe stayed close, but even he deliberately abandons her so that she won't ever suffer pain if he disappears permanently.

Holden also continues his preoccupation with sex when he meets the nuns at Grand Central and wonders how they react to "sexy" literature such as Romeo and Juliet. This encounter is indicative of Holden's earlier established Madonna/whore complex. He believes that nuns are so divorced from any sense of sexuality that they could not reasonably deal with works with erotic themes. This perhaps explains his superficial attraction to becoming a monk. The idea of compartmentalizing his sexuality and divorcing it from himself is so alluring primarily because that's what he's tried to achieve - though futilely.

However, the most significant revelation in this chapter concerns Holden's sense of class arrogance. Although he chastised Stradlater and others for their snobbery in previous chapters, Holden reveals himself to be an equal snob in this chapter, condescending to others because of their cheap suitcases. He believes that the common factor linking people is not intelligence or talent, but rather social class as defined by consumer taste. This further establishes Holden's sense of hypocrisy: although he decries the behavior of the class to which he belongs, he shares their behaviors and even accepts this value system as reasonable.

Summary and Analysis of Chapters 16-20

Chapter 16

Before meeting Sally Hayes, Holden goes to find a record called "Little Shirley Beans" for Phoebe by Estelle Fletcher. As he walks through the city, he hears a poor kid playing with his parents, singing the song "If a body catch a body coming through the rye." Hearing the song makes Holden feel less depressed.

At the theater, Holden buys tickets for I Know My Love, a play starring the Lunts. He knew that Sally would enjoy it, because it's a sophisticated show starring well-known stars. Holden goes to the Mall, where Phoebe usually plays when she is in the park, and sees a couple of kids playing there. He asks if any of them know Phoebe. They tell him that she is probably in the Museum of Natural History. Holden then reminisces about going to the Museum when he was in grade school. He remembers how he would go there often with his class, but while the exhibits would be exactly the same, he would be different each time in mind and body. Holden considers going to the museum to see Phoebe, but instead goes to the Biltmore for his date with Sally.

Chapter 17

Holden meets Sally at the Biltmore, and when he sees her he immediately feels like marrying her, even though he doesn't particularly like her. After the play, when Sally keeps mentioning that she thinks she knows people she sees, Holden replies "Why don't you go on over and give him a big soul kiss, if you know him? He'll enjoy it." Finally, Sally does go to talk to the boy she knows, George from Andover. Holden, of course, notes how phony the conversation between Sally and George is.

Holden and Sally go ice skating at Radio City, then to eat. Sally asks Holden if he is coming over to help her trim the Christmas tree. Holden asks her if she ever gets fed up. He tells her that he hates everything: taxicabs, living in New York, phony guys who call the Lunts angels. Sally tells him not to shout. He tells her that she is the only reason that he is in New York right now. If not for her, he would be in the woods, he claims. He complains about the cliques at boarding schools, and tells her that he's in lousy shape. He suggests that they borrow a car from a friend in Greenwich Village and drive up to New England where they can stay in a cabin camp until their money runs out. They could get married and live in the woods.

Sally tells him that the idea is foolish, for they are both practically children who would starve to death. She tells him that they will have a lot of time to do those things after college and marriage, but he claims that there wouldn't be "oodles" of places to go, and it would be entirely different from how she portrays it. He calls her a "royal pain in the ass," and Sally starts to cry. Holden feels somewhat guilty, and realizes that he doesn't even know where he got the idea about going to New

England.

Chapter 18

Holden once again considers giving Jane a call to invite her to go dancing. He remembers how she danced with Al Pike from Choate. Although Holden thought that he was "all muscles and no brains," Jane claimed that he had an inferiority complex and felt sorry for him. Holden thinks that girls divide guys into two types, no matter what their personality: a girl will justify bad behavior as part of an inferiority complex for those she likes, while claim those that she doesn't like are conceited.

Holden calls Carl Luce, a friend from the Whooton School who goes to Columbia, and plans to meet him that night. He then goes to the movies and is annoyed when a woman beside him becomes too emotional. The movie is a war film, which makes Holden think about D.B.'s experience in the war. D.B. hated the army, but had Holden read A Farewell to Arms, which in Holden's view celebrates soldiers. Holden thinks that if there is a war, he is glad that the atomic bomb has been invented, for he would volunteer to sit right on top of it.

Chapter 19

Holden meets Carl Luce at the Wicker Bar. Carl Luce used to gossip about people who were "flits" (homosexuals) and would tell which actors were actually gay. Holden claims that Carl was a bit "flitty" himself. When Carl arrives, he asks Holden when he is going to grow up, and is not amused by Holden's jokes. Carl is annoyed that he is having a "typical Caulfield conversation" about sex. Carl admits that he is seeing an older woman in the Village who is a sculptress from China. Holden asks questions that are too personal about Carl's sex life with his girlfriend until Carl insists that he drop the subject. Carl reminds him that the last time he saw Holden he told him to go see his father, a psychiatrist.

Chapter 20

Holden remains in the Wicker Bar getting drunk. He continues to pretend that he has been shot. Finally, he calls Sally, but her grandmother answers and asks why he is calling so late. Finally, Sally gets on the phone and realizes that Holden is drunk and quickly hangs up.

In the restroom of the Wicker Bar, Holden talks to the "flitty-looking" guy, asking if he will see the "Valencia babe" who performs there, but he tells Holden to go home. Holden finally leaves. As he walks home, Holden drops Phoebe's record and nearly starts to cry when it shatters into pieces. Forlorn, he goes to Central Park and sits down on a bench, fantasizing that he will get pneumonia and have a funeral that people have to attend. He is reassured that his parents won't let Phoebe come to his funeral because he is too young. He thinks about what Phoebe would feel if he got pneumonia and died, and figures that he should sneak home and see her, in case he does die without having a chance to say goodbye.

Analysis

In Chapter 16, although Holden can himself be a snob, he detests social pretension as manifested by the Lunts (Alfred Lunt and Joan Fontanne, considered the prominent couple in Broadway theater) and Laurence Olivier. Like so many other things, he dislikes both film and theater because they are inherently phony and, in the case of Broadway theater, validate others' notions of their own sophistication. However, Holden does not comprehend the inherent contradictions in his belief system. He rejects superficial markers of status and taste such as Broadway theater, yet in the previous chapter he used superficial markers of status (expensive suitcases) as a mark of validation.

Holden's primary interest shifts from Jane Gallagher to his sister, Phoebe. He even seems more preoccupied in seeing Phoebe than in his imminent date with Sally Hayes, for whom he has little more than contempt. The fascination that Holden has for Phoebe seems part of a longing for childhood. Holden resists change; he dislikes trips to the museum precisely because their static nature reminds him how much he changes at every visit. Holden seems to fear change and maturity, giving great sentimental weight to childish pleasures while fearing the qualities that mark adult life.

In Chapter 17, Holden's date with Sally Hayes reiterates several of the basic problems from which Holden suffers. He has intensely contradictory feelings for Sally, which even he realizes. Although he dislikes her, when he first sees her he feels that like marrying her. Holden shifts from seeming to loathe Sally to seeming to care about her, as when he proposes that they run off to New England and then calls her a pain in the ass once she refuses his offer. The confrontation between Holden and Sally in the restaurant demonstrates Holden's unreliability as a narrator. He does not realize that he is shouting at Sally Hayes through their conversation and denies it repeatedly to both the reader and to himself.

Holden's proposal is a mark of desperation, for he wishes to reject the entire society around him. He does this partially because he cannot coherently articulate what he so dislikes about the society in which he lives. Holden claims that he hates "everything," and locates this aversion in random things such as taxicabs and phonies who call the Lunts "angels." Holden even admits to himself that his actions have no logic, revealing that he does not know where he thought of escaping to New England. This continues a pattern of demonstrated behavior by Holden, while foreshadowing further desperately random actions. The New England idea also reinforces the idea that Holden stands at a difficult boundary between childhood and adulthood. Sally Hayes claims that they cannot run off together because they are still practically children, yet her rejection shows more sensible maturity than Holden's immature notions of running away from home and responsibility.

At this point, then, Holden seems trapped between his fantasy of escape and the realization that he has nowhere to go. In terms of character, he is less an anti-hero, then, then a question mark - completely trapped between motivations, unsure how to cope with the swelling pain. Thematically, Holden seems to be a singular reservoir of unexpressed pain, that has festered and turned into an anti-social soreness towards the world. But it would be a terrible mistake to take Holden as a 'rebel,' or someone who sees value in challenging society. All his rebellious thoughts and instincts are simply the products of fear, anxiety, and shame.

Holden returns to reminiscing about Jane Gallagher in Chapter 18, once again revealing his unfortunately short attention span. Soon after proposing that he and Sally Hayes run off together, Holden has already forgotten Sally and moved on to other considerations. It appears that Holden is always looking for comfort - some sort of fleeting pleasure to take away the pain which threatens to overwhelm him.

In this chapter Salinger allows Holden more coherence than usual. His cynical observations are not always misinterpretations; in some cases, he makes accurate statements about human foibles and failings. His diatribe concerning "inferiority complexes" is a particular case when Holden's suspicions have a particular coherence. He accurately finds that people have hypocritical standards of judgment for others and justify the behavior in those they like while condemning similar behavior in others. That Holden can make such observations is significant for the story, for it reinforces the idea that, although he is perpetually cynical, Holden still has the capability for intelligent and rational thought. This is a significant point, for it implies that external factors have promoted Holden's psychological difficulties and that he is not the perpetual failure that he perceives himself to be. Also, those moments when Holden shows himself to be rational make his outrageous statements more potent, such as when Holden ends his remembrance of D.B.'s war experience with the statement that he would want to sit on an atomic bomb during wartime.

Holden returns to his obsession on sex in this Chapter 19, a preoccupation that demonstrates great immaturity and a lack of propriety toward others. Holden appreciates sexuality in its most lurid forms, relishing Carl's gossip about which actors are closeted homosexuals, and can only conceive of Carl's relationship with the sculptress in terms of exotic sensuality. He even persists after Carl tells him how inappropriate his questions are, barely realizing that Carl is disgusted by Holden's behavior.

Salinger uses Holden's meeting with Carl Luce to give a more broad perspective on his behavior. Once again, this reinforces that others consider Holden to have some significant problems, but Salinger takes this viewpoint further in this chapter. Carl indicates that Holden's behavior when they meet at the Wicker Bar is typical behavior, and not the product of his altered psychological state. Holden has been suffering from his current problems since he went to Whooten with Carl Luce, and these problems have been significant; Carl even had suggested psychiatric treatment for Holden, a relatively significant recommendation in an era when therapy was highly stigmatized. Furthermore, this diagnosis comes from one of Holden's peers. This perspective on Holden's problems cannot be dismissed as easily as others, for Carl's recommendation is not the advice of the elderly Mr. Spencer or another authority figure who presumably could not understand Holden's problems.

Throughout Chapter 20, Salinger continues to foreshadow an eventual suicide attempt by Holden. Holden once again pretends that he was shot, as he did after his confrontation with Maurice, but his thoughts shift to more serious mortal concerns. He imagines his funeral as if it is an impending event, yet is curiously ambivalent about the consequences. His only concern is not whether or not he will die, but how Phoebe will react to his death. Holden's decision to visit Phoebe at the end of the chapter shows that his actions are somewhat premeditated. He approaches this visit as a means to set his affairs in order, as if he knows that he will soon die.

This fantasy, then, is reminiscent of Tom Sawyer's interruption of his own funeral - but in this case, Holden actually finds the possibility of validation and redemption in his own death. In seeming himself dead, it seems, Holden believes that he might find some instinctive motivation for continuing to live. By embracing death, maybe some glimmer of hope and conviction will stir him back to life. It never quite does, however, forcing him to invent bigger and bigger fantasies of death and people mourning him.

Otherwise, Holden continues to display more of his typical inappropriate behavior, as when he calls Sally while drunk and tries to chat with the "flitty-looking" guy. Salinger shows how Holden has become more sensitive to occurrences in this chapter. He nearly breaks down into hysterics when he breaks Phoebe's record, and it is this event that provokes his meditations on death. This foreshadows later instances in which minor events will provoke more serious catastrophes for Holden.

Summary and Analysis of Chapters 21-26

Chapter 21

Holden returns home, where he is very quiet so as not to awake his parents. Phoebe is asleep in D.B.'s room. He sits down at D.B.'s desk and looks at Phoebe's stuff, such as her math book, where she has the name "Phoebe Weatherfield Caulfield" written on the first page (her middle name is actually Josephine). Holden finally wakes up Phoebe and hugs her. Ecstatic, she tells about how she is playing Benedict Arnold in her school play. Then, she gushingly tells about how she saw a movie called The Doctor, and how their parents are out for the night. Holden shows Phoebe the broken record, and admits that he got kicked out of Pencey. Phoebe tells him that "Daddy's going to kill you," but Holden says that he is going away to a ranch in Colorado. Phoebe places a pillow over her head and refuses to talk to Holden.

Chapter 22

Phoebe tells Holden that she thinks his scheme to go out to Colorado is foolish, and asks why he failed out of yet another school. He claims that Pencey is full of phonies. He tells her about how everyone excluded Robert Ackley as a sign of how phony the students are. Holden admits that there were a couple of nice teachers, including Mr. Spencer, but then complains about the Veterans' Day ceremonies.

Phoebe tells Holden that he doesn't like anything that happens. She asks Holden for one thing that he likes a lot. He thinks of two things. The first is the nuns at Grand Central. The second is a boy at Elkton Hills named James Castle, who had a fight with a conceited guy named Phil Stabile. He threatened James, who responded by jumping out the window, killing himself. However, he tells Phoebe that he likes Allie, and he likes talking to Phoebe right now.

Finally Holden confesses to Phoebe that he would like to be a catcher in the rye: he pictures a lot of children playing in a big field of rye around the edge of a cliff. Holden imagines that he would catch them if they started to go over the cliff. Putting Phoebe back to bed, Holden decides to call up Mr. Antolini, a former teacher at Elkton Hills who now teaches English at NYU.

Chapter 23

Holden narrates that Mr. Antolini was his English teacher at Elkton Hills and was the person who carried James Castle to the infirmary. Holden and Phoebe dance to the radio, but their parents come home and Holden hides in the closet. When he believes that it is safe, Holden asks Phoebe for money and she gives him eight dollars and change. He starts to cry as he prepares to leave, which frightens Phoebe. He gives Phoebe his hunting hat and tells her that he will give her a call soon.

Chapter 24

Mr. Antolini had married an older woman who shared similar intellectual interests. When he arrives at his apartment, Holden finds Mr. Antolini in a bathrobe and slippers, drinking a highball. Holden and Mr. Antolini discuss Pencey, and Holden tells how he failed Oral Expression (debate). He tells Holden how he had lunch with his father, who told him that Holden was cutting classes and generally unprepared. He warns Holden that he is riding towards some kind of terrible fall. He says that it may be the kind where, at the age of thirty, he sits in some bar hating everyone who comes in looking as if he played football in college or hating people who use improper grammar. Furthermore, he tells Holden that the fall that he is riding for is a special and horrible kind, and that he can see Holden dying nobly for some highly unworthy cause.

He gives Holden a quote from the psychoanalyst Wilhelm Stekel: "The mark of the immature man is that he wants to die nobly for a cause, while the mark of the mature man is that he wants to live humbly for one." He finally tells Holden that once he gets past the things that annoy him, he will be able to find the kind of information that will be dear to his heart. Holden goes to sleep, and wakes up to find Mr. Antolini's hand on his head. He tells Holden that he is "simply sitting here, admiring" but Holden interrupts him, gets dressed and leaves, claiming that he has to get his bags from Grand Central Station and will be back soon.

Chapter 25

When Holden gets outside, it is getting light out. He walks over to Lexington to take the subway to Grand Central, where he slept that night. He thinks about how Mr. Antolini will explain Holden's departure to his wife. Holden feels some regret that he didn't come back to the Antolini's apartment. Holden starts reading a magazine at Grand Central; when he reads an article about hormones, he begins to worry about hormones, and worries about cancer when he reads about cancer.

As Holden walks down Fifth Avenue, he feels that he will not get to the other side of the street each time he comes to the end of a block. He feels that he will just go down somehow. Furthermore, he also makes believe that he is with Allie every time he reaches a curb. Finally, overwhelmed, Holden decides that he will go away, never go home again and never go to another prep school. He thinks he will pretend to be a deaf-mute so that he won't have to deal with stupid conversations.

Holden goes to Phoebe's school to find her and say goodbye. At the school he sees "fuck you" written on the wall, and becomes enraged as he tries to scratch it off. He writes her a note asking her to meet him near the Museum of Art so that he can return her money. While waiting for Phoebe at the Museum, Holden chats with two brothers who talk about mummies. He sees another "fuck you" written on the wall, and is convinced that someone will write that below his name on his tombstone. Holden, suffering from diarrhea, goes to the bathroom, and as he exits the bathroom he passes out. He goes unnoticed, however, and when he regains consciousness, he feels better.

Phoebe arrives, wearing Holden's hunting hat and dragging Holden's old suitcase. She tells him that she wants to come with him. She pleads ceaselessly, but Holden refuses and causes her to start crying. She throws the red hunting hat back at Holden and starts to walk away. She follows Holden to the zoo, but refuses to talk to him or get near him. He buys Phoebe a ticket for the carousel there, and watches her go around on it as "Smoke Gets in Your Eyes" plays. Afterwards, she takes back the red hunting hat and goes back on the carousel. As it starts to rain, Holden cries while watching Phoebe.

Chapter 26

Holden ends his story there. He refuses to tell what happened after he went home, descended further into sickness, and ultimately sought treatment. He says that people are concerned about whether he will apply himself next year. He tells that D.B. visits often, and he often misses Stradlater, Ackley, and even Maurice. However, he advises not to tell anybody anything, because it is the sharing of one's heart that causes a person to start missing others.

Analysis

In Chapter 21, Holden views his sister with a sense of wonder: he recounts with a sentimental appreciation each aspect of Phoebe's life, viewing her as a complete innocent. Of all the characters in The Catcher in the Rye, Phoebe is the only one that Holden treats with any degree of tenderness or respect. He listens intently to everything she says and does not react with the cynical observations that mark the rest of Holden's commentary. This is the most obvious manifestation of Holden's idealization of childhood.

However, the child Phoebe does not share her brother's views. Where Holden is sentimental, Phoebe is realistic. She realizes how angry her father will be at Holden and refuses to listen to Holden when he tells how he will go to a ranch in Colorado. Like Carl Luce, Phoebe confronts Holden with his own immaturity and lack of direction, but this criticism goes farther. Even a nine year old child can realize that Holden needs to mature, yet Holden has not come to this revelation himself.

In Chapter 22, of all of the characters in The Catcher in the Rye, Phoebe ranks with Carl Luce and Mr. Spencer as one of the most mature and perceptive. She realizes that Holden's major problem is his overwhelmingly negative attitude toward everything and everyone around him and confronts him on this attitude. When Holden talks with Phoebe, he once again reveals his hypocrisy. He laments that everyone at Pencey excluded Robert Ackley, yet Holden himself loathed Ackley, considering him boorish and obnoxious. Significantly, Holden has difficulty finding an answer to the question of what he actually likes. When he does think of a response to that question, his answers are both questionable and disturbing. That Holden appreciates the suicide of James Castle indicates his own emotional state and gives greater credence to earlier foreshadowing that Holden himself will attempt to kill himself. Holden attaches some sense of nobility to death, which he additionally shows through his idealization of Allie. This also relates to Holden's sentimental feelings about childhood. His dream of becoming a "catcher in the rye" shows that Holden has an affection for childhood. He wishes to save these children from danger so that they may frolic in the fields; one can interpret this as Holden's wish to save the children from the difficulties of adulthood.

Holden responds to Phoebe's confrontation by preparing to leave the house. This continues a pattern for Holden: he escapes responsbility, whether leaving a club early when he sees someone he dislikes or running away from boarding school. When Holden faces something that he dislikes, he cannot confront it; instead, he chooses to leave for another random destination, whether New England or Colorado.

Salinger fills in some information in Holden's biography in Chapter 23, relating Mr. Antolini to the previous story about James Castle. This serves to show Holden's thought processes. Holden's choice of Mr. Antolini seems a more desperate move once he relates it to James Castle, as if that story was more than a momentary reminder of any person who can give Holden a place to stay that night.

Holden's gift of the hunting hat to Phoebe is a significant event, for it is one of Holden's few meaningful possessions. He gives her the hunting hat as a sign that he may never see Phoebe again, whether because he has run away to Colorado or because of impending tragedy. He sets off for Mr. Antolini's, as if fully aware - even hopeful - that he may suffer the same fate as James Castle. He wants a glorious death that will end with his body taken in loving arms to a funeral where people he doesn't know will mourn him.

In Chapter 24, Mr. Antolini is the third consecutive person whom Holden encounters who forces him to confront his difficulties. Like both Carl Luce and Phoebe, Mr. Antolini senses that Holden suffers from serious problems, and definitively tells him that he is headed for a fall. However, where Mr. Antolini departs from the previous two confrontations is that he grasps the seriousness of the situation. His observation that Holden will end up having contempt for nearly everyone he meets has been made in different forms by others, yet only Mr. Antolini senses the mortal seriousness of the situation. When he quotes Wilhelm Stekel, he implies that he expects Holden to commit suicide as a form of foolish martyrdom.

Mr. Antolini is perhaps the only adult in the story whom Holden can trust and respect; Holden even does not derisively call him “old” as he does with other adults, instead referring to him by his proper title. However, like all other adults in the story, Holden feels that Mr. Antolini betrays his trust. When Holden awakens to find Mr. Antolini touching his head, he immediately concludes the worst, suspecting him of "flitty" behavior. However, Holden is a notoriously unreliable narrator, coming to

Mr. Antolini's apartment inherently suspicious of all adults and perhaps still drunk from the evening's escapades.

It seems questionable that Mr. Antolini had any malicious intent, yet Holden suspects the worst. Here is Holden's 'last adult refuge in a disintegrating world,' and yet once again Holden must escape from a situation to avoid any sort of difficult confrontation (Graham 25). Holden can now dismiss Mr. Antolini's advice to him, for he can now perceive this once-respected teacher as a predator. At the same time, if Mr. Antolini was making advances on Holden, then it's clear that perhaps Holden is right about the world - that it's incapable of offering true love, only phony attempts at connection coupled with arbitrary pain.

Holden becomes increasingly paranoid and delusional throughout Chapter 25, the last one in which he recounts his tale. Throughout this chapter he operates under the assumption that he will not survive much longer, as when he is convinced that he will not get to the other side of the street. Holden's observations become increasingly random and disjointed, as when he obsesses over profane graffiti on the school. Holden's obsession with the profanity is notable, for it shows his distaste for anything that may corrupt the innocence of children. Holden wishes to shelter children from any adult experiences, revealing his own fear of maturity. Salinger bolsters this aspect of Holden's character by concluding the chapter with Holden watching Phoebe on the carousel.

Although Holden decides to leave New York after seeing Phoebe for once last time, he has no definitive plan of action. His behavior in this chapter demonstrates a tenuous grip on sanity. Holden wishes to reject society altogether, proposing extreme ideas such as pretending to be a deaf-mute, and appears barely in control of himself throughout the chapter. His physical health begins to mirror his emotional state; he suffers from illness that renders him less than lucid and even loses consciousness. By the conclusion of this chapter, Holden finds himself completely broken down both physically and emotionally, comforted only by the sight of Phoebe and her simple, childish pleasures.

In the final chapter, Salinger leaves the actual events of Holden's presumed suicide attempt and hospitalization ambiguous; Holden only uses euphemisms such as "getting sick" to describe what has happened to him, but the implications are clear. Yet even more ambiguous than what happened to Holden is whether or not Holden will recover from his difficulties. Holden seems to harbor some sense of regret over what has happened; he claims that he even misses Stradlater and Ackley, and has used the telling of his story as a form of penitence for his behavior.

Nevertheless, while looking back on his situation Holden still harbors some of the same suspicions and deep cynicism that afflicted him throughout the novel, as shown when he dismisses the question whether or not he will apply himself. Salinger ends the novel inconclusively: he gives no strong indication what Holden has learned from his difficulties, if he has learned at all, and allows for a strong possibility that

Holden will continue his self-destructive and suicidal behavior.

Suggested Essay Questions

1. What does Holden mean when he calls people around him “phonies”?

   Answer: By “phony,” Holden means someone who is inauthentic and living on the surface as opposed to actually seeing the world clearly and living authentically, not selling out to artifice. Holden is deeply disappointed in those who cannot see beyond life's mundane duties and trivialities.
2. What is the significance of the novel’s title?

   Answer: Holden holds onto a song about a catcher in the rye who catches all the children in his path just before they run off a cliff, rescuing them from doom. Holden himself either wants to be such a catcher, who rescues children, since he believes they are the only people who are genuine in the world, or he wants to be rescued by the catcher.
3. Why does Holden slug Stradlater at Pencey?

   Answer: Holden is in love with Jane Gallagher, one of the few girls he has allowed himself to get close to. When he finds out that Stradlater had a date with her and treats the whole affair so casually, he cannot hold in his rage.
4. What is the significance of the red hunter's hat that Holden wears?

   Answer: Both Phoebe and Allie had red hair, so Holden's red hunter's cap, with its childish echoes, is his way of bonding with both of them and retaining his innocence.
5. Why does Holden ultimately leave Pencey?

   Answer: Holden is kicked out for failing too many classes, but he ultimately chooses to leave early to get away from all the phonies who are making him miserable. Specifically, he is fleeing Stradlater, who has co-opted the one and only girl he truly loves, Jane Gallagher.
6. What are some of the things that “kill” Holden, in his words?

   Answer: In general, the things that make Holden feel emotional (“killing” him) involve children. When he reads Phoebe's notebook, or when he remembers Allie's foibles, he can't block the surging emotions that overflow his defenses.
7. Why does Holden cling to the innocence of children so deeply?

   Answer: Holden has yet to recover from the stark cruelties of adulthood that so quickly stripped him of childhood innocence. Allie was taken from him cruelly, and then Holden immediately had to venture to school, where he was taunted by classmates. Holden can't see a way to regain his childhood innocence.
8. Why can't Holden force himself to sleep with the prostitute who comes to

his motel room?

Answer: Holden simply wants the comfort of someone he can talk to. He cannot bring himself to numb the loneliness and pain long enough to sleep with someone. On top of this, he is a virgin, so it is quite evident he wants his first time to be special.

9. Why does Holden finally lash out at Sally Hawkins?

   Answer: Though Sally is quite pretty and Holden enjoys having her on his arm, ultimately he cannot put up with her "phoniness." Sally cares about appearances and the superficial trappings of status, but Holden cares only about having someone he can relate to. He would rather be lonely than have to engage with a phony.

10. Why does Holden ultimately capitulate and come back home with Phoebe at the end?

    Answer: Holden wants to distance himself from people as far as possible so that he never has to experience the pain of loving someone and then losing them again. After Allie, he cannot take another heartbreak. He wants to spare himself the pain of possibly losing Phoebe or seeing her grow up by getting as far away from her as possible. But when she insists on accompanying him, Holden cannot bear to ruin her life, either by letting her come with him or by leaving without her.

Catcher in the Rye: A History of Censorship

The Catcher in the Rye has long been a lightning rod for controversy over the years, generating many calls for censorship, some of them successful, thus making it a central work in 20th-century and even censorship debates. Between 1966 and 1975, it was the most frequently banned book in schools. Teachers were fired for assigning the book to students, and numerous boards debated the book's place in the classroom.

In 1976, a legislative hearing in Oklahoma City involved a local censorship group seeking to prevent a bookseller from vending the book. The group went so far as to take vigilante action, parking a "Smutmobile" outside the hearing in the hopes of swaying the decision. Ultimately the bookseller dropped the book from his inventory in order to avoid further scandal.

Ten years later, controversy emerged again in Pennsylvania when the book was assigned in a local literature class. Parents objected, and the school board voted to ban the book. Soon after, parents in New Jersey complained to their school board about the book's "filthy and profane" language and its apparent promotion of premarital sex, homosexuality, and perversion. They also claimed that it was "explicitly pornographic" and, predictably, "immoral" (Sova 2). The board ultimately relented, banning the book for everyone but Advanced Placement students, who they ruled could understand and appreciate the novel's universal message. Still, parents were given the right to prevent their children from reading the book.

In the 1970s and 1980s, the book again became the subject of intense censorship. Parents in a small Washington town asserted that the book had nearly 800 instances of profanity. They even stated boldly that it was part of a Communist plot, one that was gaining such a foothold in the schools that "a lot of people are used [to it] and may not even be aware of it" (Sova 3). Capitalizing on anti-Communist sentiment, the parents quickly saw their complaints validated when the school board banned the book.

Objections continue to this day. Parents in Ohio, Alabama, Florida, North Dakota, California, Mississippi, Illinois, and New Hampshire have all complained to their school boards and had the book banned for a variety of reasons. Some object to the frank discussion of sexuality, others to the main character's godlessness, and some simply to the portrayal of misanthropy. Many of these parents point to the known obsessive fans of Salinger's novel, who have gone on to destructive infamy. These fans include Mark David Chapman, who assassinated John Lennon and was found carrying the book afterwards. Chapman also read a passage from the book at his sentencing. John Hinckley, Jr., who attempted to assassinate President Ronald Reagan in 1981, was also alleged to have been obsessed with the book. And Robert

John Bardo, who murdered Rebecca Schaeffer, was found carrying the book when he visited her apartment. Parents tend to call the book a sort of anti-social Bible that deserves to be exterminated from school curricula.

Author of ClassicNote and Sources

J.J. Ross, author of ClassicNote. Completed on April 23, 2000, copyright held by GradeSaver.

Updated and revised Soman Chainani and Adam Kissel, October 10, 2008 and September 30, 2009. Copyright held by GradeSaver.

Salinger, J.D. The Catcher in the Rye. Boston, MA: Little Brown, 1951.

Salzman, Jack. New Essays on Catcher in the Rye. Cambridge: Cambridge University Press, 1991.

Graham, Sarah. J.D. Salinger's The Catcher in the Rye. New York: Routledge, 2007.

Walcutt, Charles. Man's Changing Mask. Minnesota: University of Minnesota Press, 1966.

"Exploring The Catcher in the Rye." 2009-03-18. <http://www.geocities.com/exploring_citr/>.

"Catcher in the Rye Quotes." 2009-03-15. <http://www.quotegarden.com/bk-cr.html>.

"Catcher in the Rye: Research Service." 2009-03-15. <http://www.questia.com/library/literature/catcher-in-the-rye.jsp>.

Essay: The Etymology and Symbolism of Characters' Names

by Sarah Downey
May 13, 2001

Catcher in the Rye's pallid cover, adorned only with seven multicolored bands in its upper-left corner, is not what one would call eye-catching. Its reverse side lacks criticisms or reviews of any sort; in fact, it is bare of anything except a copyright date. Human beings are advised not to judge books by their covers, rather that they should look further than the obvious and try to apprehend the implied meaning. The world has peered past Catcher in the Rye's cover, cracked its pure, uniform shell of cardboard and discovered the novel of a decade, a story that has now made the name "Holden Caulfield" synonymous with "cynical adolescent." Within the novel, however, there are more "books" into which we can read a bit more deeply - the characters. It seems quite obvious that their personalities correspond with the root meanings of their names. Would brilliant author J.D. Salinger pick the name "Holden" for the protagonist without reason? Analysis uncovers connections between themes and mannerisms that are far too relevant to have been coincidental. Holden Caulfield, his younger sister Phoebe, and a cast of minor characters such as Ackley, James Castle, Carl Luce, Faith Cavendish, and Sally Hayes are several characters whose names display these connections.

As the novel opens, Holden Caulfield stands poised on a hill separating him from the rest of his school at the annual football game. He is both isolated from and above the level of his peers, watching the big game from a distance. His position is a metaphor for his views on life. The phoniness of life disgusts him, and he longs to live in a world free of the tainted hypocrisy he is seeing more and more of as he grows older. He sees the game as a collection of the "phonies" he detests, and is avoiding joining them. He is "Holden" back, not allowing himself to become a part of the ugliness he sees in virtually everyone. Chains of contempt for the world act as manacles that secure his superior attitude and ensure he will not become what he hates. The name "Holden" flawlessly portrays his inability to join society because of his high ideals for it. Caulfield, his last name, relates to recurring theme of childhood innocence. A "caul" is defined as a part of the amnion, one of the membranes enveloping the fetus, which sometimes is around the head of a child at its birth. The caul protects young children, just as Holden dreams to do when he tells Phoebe his ideal profession would be the catcher in the field of rye. Of course, the second section of his last name represents the field of rye. The few instants when Holden is genuinely happy and unaffected by his painful awakenings to the adult world deal with children, because he feels they are uncorrupted. Walking down the street in New York, Holden's rusted manacles of almost perpetual depression are unlocked when he sees a little boy singing "if a body catch a body coming through the rye." He criticizes his father, saying he wanted to appear "sharp" with the ratty hat he was wearing, and says neither parent was paying any attention to their son. He feels any adult has been demoralized, but will go to great lengths to come into any contact with a child. His perfect job, the catcher in the rye, prevents children from falling abruptly off the cliff of adulthood. He is greatly saddened by the profanity he sees on the walls of Phoebe's school because he doesn't want any children to worry about its meaning. He realizes that he cannot possibly smudge out all the profanity children are exposed to; he cannot halt their inevitable transfer into the adult world. The few characters in the novel he does not speak of negatively are those unruffled by adult phoniness- Jane, who kept her kings in the back row, "holden" back like the protagonist, the boys at the museum, Phoebe, the girl with the skate key, Allie, forever preserved a child, and the little boy singing. Holden Caulfield is held back from a society led by those whose innocence has left them as long ago as their cauls. His name illustrates more about himself than he admits.

The Catcher in the Rye had a wide array of minor characters, many of whom Holden talked to in person and others through which he merely recalled his dealings. Ackley, Holden's across the hall neighbor at Pencey, is described as:

"...one of those very, very tall, round shouldered guys - he was about 6'4- with lousy teeth. The whole time he roomed next to me, I never even once saw him brush his teeth. They always looked mossy and awful, and he damn near made you sick if you saw him in the dining room with his mouth full of mashed potatoes and peas or something. Besides that, he always had a lot of pimples. Not just on his forehead or his chin, like most guys, but all over his whole face. And not only that, he had a terrible personality. He was also sort of a nasty guy. I wasn't too crazy about him, to tell you the truth."

Holden's blunt description disgusts the reader and provides a clear, graphic account of Ackley. The name "Ackley" sounds like acne, one of Ackley's more prominent features. It also sounds similar to a reaction of disgust. When hurt, humans use "ouch" as an exclamation of their pain; when disgusted, we tend to make an "ecch" or "ack" noise. Ackley's loathsome features could evoke this type of reaction. Ackley frustrated and disgusted Holden, but even in his distaste for his roommate, Holden still concluded the novel saying that he misses him. James Castle's last name is pertinent to his high ideals. He is in a castle, above his insincere peers. He refused to take back an insult even while being tortured by a group of boys, and committed suicide before he would apologize for his comment. James plunged out of his window to his death, or out of his castle of higher ideals. The word "castle" brings to mind great heights; kings were above their subjects both in the height of their dwelling and in their power. The character of James Castle also relates to the theme of falling throughout the story- Holden's gradual fall of health to fanaticizing falling to his death after Maurice attacks him. Holden admires Carl Luce because of his intelligence, saying he had the highest IQ of anyone at The Whooton School. He says he does not like him too much, but he was very intellectual, citing his IQ as the only reason why he was worth talking to. Carl's last name, "Luce", means "light" in Spanish. Knowledge is the light of life, ignorance the darkness. Carl's last name illustrates the quality for which Holden most respects him. Faith Cavendish's character expands on Holden's beliefs that he can appear older and more mature than his actual age. He believes he can give the impression of greater age by his gray hair, height, and incessant drinking and smoking, although he does not seem to realize that he is the only person who thinks he can pass for 21. Holden smoked a great deal of cigarettes at the Edmont and then decided to call Faith Cavendish. His smoking symbolizes his struggle to seem older. When he called, he lowered his voice to conceal his age as well. Faith's last name is defined as leaf tobacco softened, sweetened, and pressed into plugs or cakes. It is certainly not by chance that the very thing Holden does excessively to conceal his age around women is Faith's last name. Sally Hayes is a shallow socialite Holden used to date before he attended Pencey. He says he used to think she was intelligent, because she knew quite a lot about the theatre and literature, but when enough time went by he saw she was lacking in intelligence. He says "My big trouble is, I always sort of think whoever I'm necking is a pretty intelligent person. It hasn't got a goddamn thing to do with it, but I keep thinking it anyway." Even after reflecting on her stupidity, he was struck dumb by her looks. "The funny part is, I felt like marrying her the minute I saw her. I'm crazy. I didn't even like her much, and yet all of a sudden I felt like I was in love with her and wanted to marry her. I swear to god I'm crazy. I admit it." Holden is aware of his actual feelings towards her even as he feels an intense, sudden attraction to her. Her last names, Hayes, shows the phony haze even Holden himself becomes lost in due to her looks.

Holden's love for children first shows itself in his description of his young sister, Phoebe. All of his thoughts up to those of his sister are dark and unsettling. Phoebe's description is so outrightly loving that the reader is shown an entirely new side to Holden, one that shows he is not entirely incapable of happiness. Phoebe's role as a minor character in the novel is to keep Holden anchored to reality; to prevent him from ruining his life completely and losing all hope in his future. It is because of his fear of what Phoebe would do without him that keeps Holden from moving out west. When she tries to accompany him, Holden implicitly realizes that the trip west would destroy Phoebe's innocence, and that his erratic behavior would prove harmful to her. He makes the decision to stay to comfort Phoebe and to keep her from falling over the cliff by the rye field before her time. Phoebe is the light countering Holden's overwhelming dark depression. Her name is a species of bird known for flicking its tail and hopping about. Phoebe is skinny, "but a good skinny, a roller skate type of skinny," who is in constant motion- dancing, laughing, writing stories, talking about her friends. The word "phoebe" also means "shining" when traced to its old English roots. In mythology, Phoebe was a Titaness who became identified with Artemis as goddess of the moon. All three of the meanings relate to heavenly heights. Phoebe shines as the light in Holden's life, bringing him pure joy when nothing else possibly can. As the moon orbits the earth, Phoebe is always in Holden's thoughts, affecting his decisions for the better, subconsciously holding him back from blindly stumbling off the cliff of the rye field.

From the etymology of "luce" to "light" to Phoebe's name conveying shining, it is apparent there is much beneath the surface of J.D. Salinger's character's titles.

Whether he intended for Holden's last name to signify his love for preserving innocence has been disputed, but its meaning cannot be more obvious than if it were written out for the reader. Books cannot be judged by their covers; doing so would show phony qualities Holden despises and limit the reader's understanding of what is available to them. In both reading and living, one must delve at times to see intended meaning. To achieve the greatest knowledge of The Catcher in the Rye, the reader must examine the many levels of meaning associated with the character's names.

Essay: The Maturation of Holden Caulfield and Henry Fleming

by Sarah Downey
June 21, 2002

The Catcher in the Rye and The Red Badge of Courage detail the gradual maturation of two immature boys into self-reliant young men. The steady speed at which Salingerís and Craneís language streams enables the reader to see the independent events that lead up to the ultimate rite of passage for both Henry and Holden. Although the pinnacle of maturity Holden reached concerned his pessimistic view of the world and Henryís was a unifying moment of bravery, both boys experienced an epiphany over the course of their respective tales. Holden came to a realization in the timeless peace of an Egyptian tomb that forced him to reevaluate his immature and selfish views. His new attitude was first displayed while he watched Phoebe snatch at the gold rings of the Central Park carousel. Henry found his manhood during the fierce chaos of battle. These final rites of passage differ in particulars, but their underlying themes possess many similarities.

As The Catcher in the Rye progresses, Holden comes to terms that he is powerless to rid the world of evil and forever protect both young children and himself from growing up. Although his perception of the world as a corrupt and phony place is not modified significantly, his final realization is a tremendous step towards accepting the inevitable- he must mature eventually, and the world will never be pure. The enlightenment itself is a step towards manhood. His epiphany occurs after spotting another "fuck you" etched in the serene Egyptian tomb. Holden sees he cannot escape perversion even in the ancient vault. He grasps that he cannot possible go about the world erasing all the profanity scrawled throughout it; eventually, every child is going to have to be concerned and upset as they come to terms with its meaning. They must grow up one day, as he knows he must as well. Salinger follows up Holdenís epiphany with several supporting events. Holden has a nervous breakdown because he now knows with an abrupt and sickening certainty that he is unable to stop both evil and maturation. His emotional outpouring at the merry-go-round further sustains his prior reasoning that he cannot stop maturation.

"All the kids kept trying to grab for the gold ring, and so was old Phoebe, and I was sort of afraid she'd fall off the goddam horse, but I didn't say anything or do anything. The thing with kids is, if they want to grab for the gold ring, you have to let them do it, and not say anything. If they fall off, they fall off, but it's bad if you say anything to them."

He knows that he cannot catch them with his net spun of dreams- they will eventually have to experience a fall. Itís part of growing up. Upon seeing this, Holden himself has developed.

Henry Fleming enlists as a youth with heroic fantasies of battle lingering in his mind and walks off the "place of blood and wrath" three days later a serene veteran of battle. He came from hot plowshares seeking a Homeric Iliad, timid and anxious about his potential and what others think of him. He ponders a great dilemma: will he run from battle? He is reassured after asking the tall soldier his question. His friend tells him that he would do what the rest of the regiment was doing. Henry is not an individual yet, he is a fragment of a mass of men. Henry feels as though running from the backlash of the first skirmish he fought was a great debacle, and he is further tormented when the tattered soldier asks him how he got his feigned wound. He is haunted by pangs of guilt. As he participates in more battles, the opposition grows more and more human, as opposed to the monsters he envisioned them to be earlier. He sees them as human when he experiences his first surge of fierce, animalian anger. Henryís epiphany occurs in the following "battle". He discards the expectations of his peers and declares his individuality and courage by seizing the flag from the dead color sergeant and waving it before the regiment. He risks death as the easiest of targets and thus displays his courage and strength. The seizing of the flag is Henryís ultimate rite of passage. He discards the terrified and cautious youth he enlisted as and becomes a mature, courageous adult. His reach for the flag proves he is as brave and courageous as the warriors whose stories dazzled him as a boy.

Henry and Holden began both their stories weaker and more ignorant than they left them. How are their rises to maturity similar and different? Both stories cover a time period of about three days. The three days are greatly important, as they detail the rite of passage from youth to maturity. Such a prodigious transformation in a mere three days implies an extraordinary sequence of preceding events. Both The Catcher in the Rye and The Red Badge of Courage tell a story of one of the most relevant time periods in both of the main characterís lives- their rise to adulthood. Both characters seem to have promising futures ahead of them. Holden ends his account of "the madman stuff" that happened to him last Christmas giving the impression that he will try harder in school and that he actually missed the people he criticized so harshly. Henryís story closes as he strolls through a landscape he now appreciates. The concluding sentence, "over the river a golden ray of sun came through the hosts of leaden rain clouds," is an almost romantic depiction of the bright future Henry has before him. The language the authors use to convey the story differs. In The Catcher in the Rye, Holden himself describes the events. The language is down to earth and flows easily, exactly as if the reader were sitting and listening to Holden instead of the psychiatrist. Because Holden told his story in one sitting, there is no prominent change in language over the course of the story. In The Red Badge of Courage, a narrator tells Henryís tale. Figurative language and a vivid use of color support the narration. The story opened with a paragraph darkened with ominous red and black shading and ended on a blissful golden tone, illustrating Henryís rise to maturity even through colorization. The narration also differs in that Henryís narrator is impartial to the story, whereas Holden clearly attempts to alter certain facts in his favor. For example, when he and Sally are talking, Holden speaks as though Sally was a bit mixed up and that he was in fact speaking in a normal tone of voice.

However, the reader can still manage to detect this falsity from his frenzied narration. The Red Badge of Courageís narrator does not try to shield events out of shame or haste; the story is much more straightforward. Again, Holdenís immaturity is displayed through narration as he scrambles to hide his embarrassment.

The rise to adulthood is a common theme explored by authors. The path from youth to maturity can be prodigious in its complexity and length, but Salinger and Crane have each provided an account of this nature that occurred over only three days. Fueled by the strength they acquired after overcoming personal barriers, the protagonists reached maturity through their own epiphanies. Henry found his in the dignity he wished to uphold for himself and his regiment, and Holden in a pitiful realization that he is powerless to change the world. The price Henry and Holden paid for their maturity was a loss of much of the egocentricity they had possessed. As Tolstoy said, "everyone thinks of changing the world, but no one thinks of changing himself."

Quiz 1

1. **Where does the title of the novel come from?**
   A. a poem by Robert Burns
   B. the title of Holden's favorite song
   C. a game that Holden and Allie would play
   D. a reference to Greek mythology

2. **What is the name of the benefactor of Holden's dormitory wing?**
   A. Fawcett
   B. Merriman
   C. Weiss
   D. Ossenburger

3. **What is Phoebe's favorite movie?**
   A. The Wizard of Oz
   B. The Doctor
   C. The 39 Steps
   D. Gone With the Wind

4. **After his fight with Stradlater, Holden claims that he is a/an ________.**
   A. sadist
   B. pacifist
   C. anarchist
   D. wimp

5. **Holden tells the girls he saw ________ at the Lavender Room.**
   A. Laurence Olivier
   B. Alfred Lunt
   C. Gary Cooper
   D. Peter Lorre

6. **What is one of Holden's least favorite words?**
   A. indeed
   B. fabulous
   C. grand
   D. phony

7. **Which prep school did Holden NOT attend?**
   A. Pencey
   B. Andover
   C. Whooton
   D. Elkton Hills

8. **How did Allie die?**
   A. a car accident
   B. leukemia
   C. World War II
   D. polio

9. **Which of the following things does Holden NOT like?**
   A. Hemingway's "A Farewell to Arms"
   B. Allie Caulfield
   C. The nuns at Grand Central
   D. James Castle

10. **What smell permeates Mr. Spencer's home?**
   A. Alcohol
   B. Vicks Nose Drops
   C. Potpourri
   D. Cigar Smoke

11. **Which of these statements is not true?**
   A. Holden dislikes Stradlater because he is a "secret slob."
   B. Holden dislikes Ernest Morrow because he is so well-respected.
   C. Holden dislikes Ackley because he is a slob.
   D. Holden dislikes Dick Slagle because of his cheap suitcases.

12. **In what month does the novel take place?**
   A. January
   B. December
   C. November
   D. May

13. **Why does Holden believe that everyone mistakes him for an older person?**
    A. He has a perpetual five-o'clock shadow.
    B. He has prematurely graying hair.
    C. He is 6'4".
    D. He uses obscure French words and phrases.

14. **Which sentence about Carl Luce's girlfriend is not true?**
    A. She is Chinese.
    B. She is older than Carl.
    C. She lives in Brooklyn.
    D. She is a sculptress.

15. **According to Holden, which item shows that Stradlater is a phony?**
    A. his suitcases
    B. his razor
    C. his hound's-tooth jacket
    D. his baseball mitt

16. **Why does Holden dislike museums?**
    A. Museums remind him of Allie
    B. Only phonies who want to appear intellectual visit museums
    C. Never changing, they remind Holden of other changes
    D. Holden's mother works in a museum

17. **Which of the following was not one of Holden's teachers?**
    A. Vinson
    B. Spencer
    C. Antolini
    D. Luce

18. **After Holden fights Stradlater, what does he think about?**
    A. Joining a monastery.
    B. Jumping out a window.
    C. Shooting Stradlater.
    D. Moving to a ranch in Colorado.

19. **Which character does Holden talk to during the course of the novel?**
    A. Jane Gallagher
    B. Faith Cavendish
    C. D.B. Caulfield
    D. Hazle Weatherfield

20. **Where does Holden get drunk?**
    A. Ernie's
    B. Lavender Room
    C. Wicker Bar
    D. Edmond Hotel

21. **Which of the following characters symbolizes childhood innocence for Holden?**
    A. Robert Ackley
    B. Allie Caulfield
    C. Lillian Simmons
    D. D.B. Caulfield

22. **Which of the following items best symbolizes adulthood for Holden?**
    A. Little Shirley Beans record
    B. Red hunting hat
    C. Vicks Nose Drops
    D. Toenail clipper

23. **What is the significance of Stradlater's razor?**
    A. shows how the conceited Stradlater is actually a slob
    B. symbolizes adulthood
    C. symbolizes the violence of adulthood
    D. foreshadows how Holden will attempt suicide

24. **Who does not symbolize Holden's views of sex?**
    A. Faith Cavendish
    B. the guests at the Edmond Hotel
    C. Mrs. Antolini
    D. Sunny

25. **Which of the following statements about Jane Gallagher is not true?**

A. Her relationship with her stepfather represents Holden's distrust of adult authority.

B. She represents Holden's contempt for phoniness.

C. She represents Holden's inability to conceive of women as anything but entirely pure or entirely corrupt.

D. She represents innocent gender relations for Holden.

Quiz 1 Answer Key

1. **(A)** a poem by Robert Burns
2. **(D)** Ossenburger
3. **(C)** The 39 Steps
4. **(B)** pacifist
5. **(C)** Gary Cooper
6. **(C)** grand
7. **(B)** Andover
8. **(B)** leukemia
9. **(A)** Hemingway's "A Farewell to Arms"
10. **(B)** Vicks Nose Drops
11. **(B)** Holden dislikes Ernest Morrow because he is so well-respected.
12. **(B)** December
13. **(B)** He has prematurely graying hair.
14. **(C)** She lives in Brooklyn.
15. **(B)** his razor
16. **(C)** Never changing, they remind Holden of other changes
17. **(D)** Luce
18. **(A)** Joining a monastery.
19. **(B)** Faith Cavendish
20. **(C)** Wicker Bar
21. **(B)** Allie Caulfield
22. **(C)** Vicks Nose Drops
23. **(A)** shows how the conceited Stradlater is actually a slob
24. **(D)** Sunny
25. **(B)** She represents Holden's contempt for phoniness.

Quiz 2

1. **Holden's stories illustrate all of the following themes except**
   A. suicide as a healing measure
   B. innocence of childhood
   C. threatening adult authority
   D. Holden's dysfunctional attitudes about sex

2. **"I can very clearly see you dying nobly, one way or another, for some highly unworthy cause." This idea that Mr. Antolini expresses to Holden illustrates which of the following themes?**
   A. suicide as an escape from Holden's problems
   B. death as the only way to preserve childhood
   C. martyrdom as a noble sacrifice
   D. violence as a mark of adulthood

3. **Who does NOT evoke the theme of phoniness for Holden?**
   A. Joe Yale
   B. Carl Luce
   C. The Lunts
   D. Mr. Haas

4. **Which of the following best illustrates that Holden is in part a hypocrite?**
   A. Phoebe's Little Shirley Beans record
   B. Dick Slagle's suitcases
   C. Holden's red hunting hat
   D. Sally Hayes' Christmas tree

5. **Which of the following does not foreshadow a suicide attempt by Holden?**
   A. the confrontation between Holden and Sally
   B. pneumonia
   C. James Castle
   D. the line by Wilhelm Stekel

6. **What is the best interpretation of Mr. Antolini's behavior toward Holden?**
   A. Mr. Antolini is a repressed homosexual who is having an affair with Carl Luce.
   B. Like all of the adults Holden meets, Mr. Antolini is a dangerous sexual predator.
   C. Holden is so paranoid and suspicious of others that he automatically suspects the worst from Mr. Antolini.
   D. The drunk and delusional Holden has a hallucination; the event never

actually happened.

7. **Holden's encounter with Lillian Simmons illustrates which of the following themes?**
   A. Holden's inability to confront things that he dislikes.
   B. Holden's idealization of childhood.
   C. Holden's inability to deal maturely with female sexuality.
   D. Holden's contempt for anybody who does not belong to the same social class.

8. **Which of the following best symbolizes the transition from childhood to adulthood?**
   A. Stradlater's seduction of Jane Gallagher.
   B. The gold ring on the carousel.
   C. Carl Luce's criticism of Holden.
   D. Holden's proposal to Sally Hayes.

9. **Which is the best interpretation of Holden's use of pseudonyms?**
   A. Holden fears that people will learn who he is and send him back to Pencey.
   B. Holden hates his family and thus wants to relinquish the Caulfield name.
   C. Holden is ashamed of who he is and tries to hide his identity.
   D. Holden has contempt for others who are foolish enough to believe his lies.

10. **All of the following are significant about Holden's essay for Stradlater except ________.**
   A. It shows that Stradlater is so self-centered that he thinks Holden will automatically write it for him.
   B. It shows that Holden is the only one who remembers Allie's death.
   C. It shows that Holden is respected as an intelligent, talented writer despite his poor grades.
   D. It shows that Holden is still preoccupied with his brother's death.

11. **Which character does not assess Holden's problems with some degree of accuracy?**
   A. Carl Luce
   B. Phoebe Caulfield
   C. Mr. Antolini
   D. Stradlater

12. **What word does Holden use to describe sex?**
   A. crumby
   B. disappointing
   C. mysterious
   D. phony

13. **Which of the following is a possible explanation why Holden started to distrust adults?**
    A. Mr. Cudahy
    B. Mr. Spencer
    C. Mr. Antolini
    D. D.B. Caulfield

14. **What is significant about Holden claiming to be 22?**
    A. Holden believes that if he pretends to be older, women will like him much more.
    B. Holden believes that he can pass for 22, but others easily realize that he is actually much younger.
    C. Holden claims to be the age Allie would actually be if he had lived.
    D. Holden claims to be 22 because he is so eager to be accepted as a mature adult.

15. **All of the following could describe both Holden Caulfield and Stradlater except ________.**
    A. self-centered
    B. arrogant
    C. conceited
    D. phony

16. **What is Holden's standard response to any difficulty he faces?**
    A. He reacts violently, lashing out on anybody who provokes him.
    B. He does not face the situation and instead leaves.
    C. He breaks down into tears, apologizing for his mistakes without any real penitence.
    D. He refuses to back down, even when he knows he is wrong.

17. **Which of the following is not significant about Carl Luce?**
    A. He illustrates Holden's preoccupation with sex.
    B. He shows that Holden's mental problems are deeper and more significant than originally implied.
    C. Unlike the other characters who criticize Holden, Carl is one of Holden's peers.
    D. He has suffered through problems similar to Holden's and shows how one can get better.

18. **Based on the events of the novel, which character best articulates Salinger's view of Holden?**
    A. Robert Ackley
    B. Maurice
    C. Phoebe Caulfield
    D. Mr. Antolini

19. **Holden envisions death by all of the following methods except _________.**

A. suicide
B. leukemia
C. pneumonia
D. nuclear war

20. **Which is the best interpretation of Sally's reaction to Holden's proposal?**

A. She is disgusted that Holden wants to act like an adult so soon.

B. She does not even consider the idea that she would go to a place where she could not see the Lunts' plays.

C. She thinks that Holden is confused, but she does not comprehend the seriousness of his difficulties.

D. She thinks that Holden's idea is laughable and dismisses it as a joke.

21. **Based on the final chapter, what is most likely to occur to Holden after the end of the novel?**

A. He will regret his decisions for the rest of his life, always feeling guilty.

B. He will find great solace in therapy and antidepressants.

C. He may learn something from his difficulties and "apply himself," but he probably will continue to make similar mistakes.

D. He will make a full recovery and return to Pencey by next term.

22. **Which of the following is not significant about Bernice Krebs?**

A. Holden neither likes her nor respects her and appreciates her only as a sex object.

B. Holden dislikes her because she has enthusiasm for seeing tourist attractions, while Holden cannot conceive of a person reasonably being excited about anything.

C. Holden finds her interchangeable with her two friends and cannot see her as an individual.

D. Holden attempts to pretend that he is older around her, but she immediately sees through him.

23. **Which of the following does not symbolize some aspect of childhood in the story?**

A. Jane Gallagher
B. Sally Hayes
C. the red hunting hat
D. the carousel

24. **Which of the following is not significant about the carousel?**

A. Phoebe's attempt to reach the gold ring on the carousel shows that she is trying to grow up.

B. Holden can only watch the carousel, but he is so isolated from others that he cannot ride on it with Phoebe.

C. The carousel reminds Holden of the innocence of childhood.

D. The carousel always plays the same songs, and it thus reassures Holden that some things do not change.

25. **Which of the following is not true about D.B. Caulfield?**
   A. He is dating an English actress.
   B. He is a war veteran.
   C. He was engaged to Lillian Simmons.
   D. He works as a screenwriter in Hollywood.

Quiz 2 Answer Key

1. **(A)** suicide as a healing measure
2. **(A)** suicide as an escape from Holden's problems
3. **(B)** Carl Luce
4. **(B)** Dick Slagle's suitcases
5. **(A)** the confrontation between Holden and Sally
6. **(C)** Holden is so paranoid and suspicious of others that he automatically suspects the worst from Mr. Antolini.
7. **(A)** Holden's inability to confront things that he dislikes.
8. **(B)** The gold ring on the carousel.
9. **(D)** Holden has contempt for others who are foolish enough to believe his lies.
10. **(B)** It shows that Holden is the only one who remembers Allie's death.
11. **(D)** Stradlater
12. **(A)** crumby
13. **(A)** Mr. Cudahy
14. **(B)** Holden believes that he can pass for 22, but others easily realize that he is actually much younger.
15. **(C)** conceited
16. **(B)** He does not face the situation and instead leaves.
17. **(D)** He has suffered through problems similar to Holden's and shows how one can get better.
18. **(D)** Mr. Antolini
19. **(B)** leukemia
20. **(C)** She thinks that Holden is confused, but she does not comprehend the seriousness of his difficulties.
21. **(C)** He may learn something from his difficulties and "apply himself," but he probably will continue to make similar mistakes.
22. **(C)** Holden finds her interchangeable with her two friends and cannot see her as an individual.
23. **(B)** Sally Hayes
24. **(B)** Holden can only watch the carousel, but he is so isolated from others that he cannot ride on it with Phoebe.
25. **(C)** He was engaged to Lillian Simmons.

Quiz 3

1. **What is significant about Holden's dislike of the graffiti on the school wall?**
   A. It takes little for Holden to lapse into insane behavior.
   B. Holden wants to protect a sense of innocence in children.
   C. Holden is hallucinating. He does not remember that he actually wrote the graffiti on the wall.
   D. Holden is a hypocrite, for he hates profanity but uses it himself in most conversations.

2. **Where is Stradlater's date waiting for him?**
   A. the car
   B. the cafeteria
   C. the yard
   D. the Annex

3. **Holden originally promised to pay the hooker how much money for her services?**
   A. 10 bucks
   B. 20 bucks
   C. 30 bucks
   D. 5 bucks

4. **Who does Holden call drunkenly?**
   A. his mother
   B. Jane
   C. Sally
   D. Mrs. Antolini

5. **If there's one word that Holden hates, what is it?**
   A. junked
   B. lady
   C. grand
   D. broke

6. **What's the name of Phoebe's fictional heroine she writes into her stories?**
   A. Dree Meringer
   B. John Caulfield
   C. Pepper Pippens
   D. Hazel Weatherfield

7. **What's the name of the pimp who demands money from Holden for his time with the hooker?**
   A. Maurice
   B. Jake
   C. Sunny
   D. Daniel

8. **What nickname does Maurice give Holden?**
   A. master
   B. bud
   C. chief
   D. kiddo

9. **What is the name of Holden's current prep school?**
   A. Spence
   B. Pencey
   C. Chatham
   D. Jefferson

10. **What's Old Luce's relationship to Holden?**
   A. teacher
   B. parole officer
   C. trustee
   D. student advisor

11. **Who is Phoebe playing in her school Christmas pageant?**
   A. Tiny Tim
   B. Benedict Arnold
   C. Santa Claus
   D. Jesus Christ

12. **When Holden flees the Antolinis, where does he say he has to go?**
   A. back to school
   B. to Japan
   C. home
   D. the station

13. **Where does Holden tell Phoebe to meet him before he leaves for good?**
    A. Zoo
    B. Home
    C. Annex
    D. Museum of Art

14. **What course does Holden say he flunked at Pence?**
    A. English
    B. Home Economics
    C. Moral Reasoning
    D. Oral Expression

15. **What does Holden call Sally that makes her freak out?**
    A. a holy terror
    B. a bitch
    C. royal pain in the ass
    D. a piece of work

16. **What does Holden drop that breaks into fifty pieces?**
    A. Phoebe's record
    B. Sally's necklace
    C. Phoebe's snowglobe
    D. Sally's tiara

17. **What's Phoebe's real middle name?**
    A. Heather
    B. Josephine
    C. Jemma
    D. Henry

18. **What does Phoebe say her middle name is?**
    A. Weatherfield
    B. Meringen
    C. Antolini
    D. Luce

19. **Which boy committed suicide at Elkton Hills?**
    A. Carter Weatherfield
    B. Macon Braga
    C. James Castle
    D. John Beggins

20. **Which religious group does Holden accuse of being too insular?**
    A. Hindus
    B. Catholics
    C. Islamists
    D. Jews

21. **At which school did Holden and Raymond Goldfarb abscond to drink Scotch?**
    A. Pencey
    B. Chatham
    C. Elton Hills
    D. The Whooten School

22. **Who is the headmaster at Pencey?**
    A. Pencey
    B. Maurice
    C. Thurmer
    D. Luce

23. **What does Holden use as a fake name?**
    A. Joseph Biggins
    B. Rudolf Schmidt
    C. Mason Dixon
    D. James Weatherfield

24. **Who is Rudolph Schmidt in actuality?**
    A. the train conductor
    B. the gym trainer
    C. the dorm advisor
    D. the school janitor

25. **What word does Holden use to describe a gay man?**
   A. flitty
   B. fruity
   C. faggy
   D. poofy

Quiz 3 Answer Key

1. **(B)** Holden wants to protect a sense of innocence in children.
2. **(D)** the Annex
3. **(D)** 5 bucks
4. **(C)** Sally
5. **(C)** grand
6. **(D)** Hazel Weatherfield
7. **(A)** Maurice
8. **(C)** chief
9. **(B)** Pencey
10. **(D)** student advisor
11. **(B)** Benedict Arnold
12. **(D)** the station
13. **(D)** Museum of Art
14. **(D)** Oral Expression
15. **(C)** royal pain in the ass
16. **(A)** Phoebe's record
17. **(B)** Josephine
18. **(A)** Weatherfield
19. **(C)** James Castle
20. **(B)** Catholics
21. **(D)** The Whooten School
22. **(C)** Thurmer
23. **(B)** Rudolf Schmidt
24. **(D)** the school janitor
25. **(A)** flitty

Quiz 4

1. **What kind of glass does Mr. Antolini drink out of?**
   A. Scotch
   B. martini
   C. highball
   D. shot

2. **Who are the stars of the show that Holden takes Sally to?**
   A. the Carpenters
   B. the Lunts
   C. the Broods
   D. the Trappers

3. **What's the name of Holden's brother?**
   A. Andrew
   B. Joseph
   C. D.B.
   D. Paul

4. **What is the name of D.B.'s ex whom Holden runs into?**
   A. Anna Stradlater
   B. Lillian Simpson
   C. Jane Weatherfield
   D. Sally Caplan

5. **Who does Stradlater have a date with, incurring Holden's wrath?**
   A. Sally Johnson
   B. Jane Gallagher
   C. Kerry Washington
   D. Mahona Luce

6. **How old does Holden tell the hooker he is?**
   A. 16
   B. 18
   C. 22
   D. 25

7. **What does Holden normally have for breakfast?**
   A. coffee
   B. biscuit
   C. bacon
   D. orange juice

8. **Who does Holden ultimately go on a date with?**
   A. Sally Johnson
   B. Sally Renninger
   C. Sally Hayes
   D. Sally Weatherfield

9. **What holiday does Holden make fun of at Pencey?**
   A. Labor Day
   B. Election Day
   C. Memorial Day
   D. Veterans' Day

10. **How does Phoebe spell her imaginary name?**
   A. Hayzel
   B. Hayzle
   C. Hazle
   D. Hazel

11. **Who is Ed Banky?**
   A. Tennis Partner at Pencey
   B. Basketball Coach at Pencey
   C. Superintendent at Pencey
   D. Tailor in Chappaqua

12. **Who are Marco and Miranda?**
   A. actors
   B. dancers
   C. hookers
   D. barmaids

13. **Where does Holden want to travel with Phoebe?**
    A. Massachusetts
    B. California
    C. India
    D. Canada

14. **Harris Macklin was Holden's roommate where?**
    A. Pencey
    B. Whooton
    C. Horace Mann
    D. Elkton Hills

15. **Holden is concerned about the migration of which animals in the winter?**
    A. pigeons
    B. elephants
    C. ducks
    D. swans

16. **Which one of these is not one of Holden's fake monikers?**
    A. Rudolph Schmidt
    B. Mr. Caulfield
    C. Jason Latham
    D. James Steele

17. **Who was "once" Catholic?**
    A. Holden's grandfather
    B. Holden's grandmother
    C. Holden's father
    D. Holden's mother

18. **What does Holden say ends up making you blue as hell no matter what?**
    A. family
    B. love
    C. boys
    D. money

19. **What is the name of the putrid band that Holden hears in the bar?**
A. Murray Carney
B. Dimitri
C. John Weatherfield
D. Buddy Singer

20. **What "kills" Holden about children?**
A. their notebooks
B. their hair
C. their eyes
D. their shoes

21. **Where does Holden arrange to meet Sally?**
A. at the Biltmore
B. at the Zoo
C. at the House
D. at the Museum

22. **What did Holden once play with Jane Gallagher?**
A. tennis
B. checkers
C. backgammon
D. chess

23. **Which condition does Allie not have?**
A. sinus trouble
B. halitosis
C. staph infections
D. lousy teeth

24. **What kind of dog did Jane Gallagher have?**
A. poodle
B. pitbull
C. cocker spaniel
D. doberman

25. **Stradlater beats Holden up because Holden asks him if he did what with Jane Gallagher?**
    A. Gave her a kiss
    B. Gave her a big one
    C. Gave her the time
    D. Gave her trouble

Quiz 4 Answer Key

1. **(C)** highball
2. **(B)** the Lunts
3. **(C)** D.B.
4. **(B)** Lillian Simpson
5. **(B)** Jane Gallagher
6. **(C)** 22
7. **(D)** orange juice
8. **(C)** Sally Hayes
9. **(D)** Veterans' Day
10. **(C)** Hazle
11. **(B)** Basketball Coach at Pencey
12. **(B)** dancers
13. **(A)** Massachusetts
14. **(D)** Elkton Hills
15. **(C)** ducks
16. **(C)** Jason Latham
17. **(C)** Holden's father
18. **(D)** money
19. **(D)** Buddy Singer
20. **(A)** their notebooks
21. **(A)** at the Biltmore
22. **(B)** checkers
23. **(C)** staph infections
24. **(D)** doberman
25. **(C)** Gave her the time

15913953R00068

Printed in Poland
by Amazon Fulfillment
Poland Sp. z o.o., Wrocław